You've Been Lied To!

Revealing Truth so You Can Heal, Grow and Help Others Do the Same.

—

Matthew Rodante

Discovering
TRUTH PRESS

"If you don't know the truth, you will die with the lie."

- Nick Vujicic

To those who hunger for Truth.
May you be satisfied.

Contents

Introduction

This 19th century legend below is perhaps more relevant today than when it first began making rounds some 200 years ago.

The Truth and the Lie meet one day.

The Lie says to the Truth: "It's a marvelous day today!" The Truth looks up to the skies and sighs, for the day was really beautiful. They spend a lot of time together, ultimately arriving beside a well.

The Lie tells the Truth: "The water is very nice, let's take a bath together!" The Truth, once again suspicious, tests the water and discovers that it indeed is very nice. They undress and start bathing.

Suddenly, the Lie comes out of the water, puts on the clothes of the Truth and runs away. The furious Truth comes out of the well and runs everywhere to find the Lie and to get her clothes back.

The World, seeing the Truth naked, turns its gaze away, with contempt and rage. The poor Truth returns to the well and disappears forever, hiding therein, its shame.

Since then, the Lie travels around the world, dressed as the Truth, satisfying the needs of society, because, the World, in any case, harbors no wish at all to meet the naked Truth.[2]

In my opinion, this legend describes our society exactly...up until the very last line. While there are people who don't care much for the truth because it might make them uncomfortable, in my experience, many people, especially young adults, are hungry for the truth.

When I grew up, I thought I was smart. Heck, I scored really well on the SAT (yeah, the SAT) when I was in high school. I also had pretty good grades and some other accolades.

Then came college. I was no longer the smartest one in the room. In fact, I often found the room *full* of people smarter than me. Having learned so much, yet there was so much more to learn. Ironically, it seemed the more I learned, the more I realized how little I knew and the more I had to question everything I had already learned up to that point. There was evidence to support much of my knowledge, but there was also evidence that contradicted many things I had been told or believed. I began to realize that many things I had thought were true, weren't.

Our society has evolved to hit people with thousands of daily messages, directly or indirectly, many of which are lies. Often, these lies were obvious, but not always.

These lies came from all sorts of people and places. Many lies came from society. Many lies came from people who were jealous, angry, arrogant or hurt. Some of the lies came from close friends. A few lies came from myself, like after a traumatic experience or after a successful accomplishment.

Most of the lies, however, came from the media. Whether it was the countless ads on tv, in magazines, on billboards, in the newspaper or just from the media I consumed, I received hundreds of messages weekly, and many of them were lies. With computers, the internet, smart tvs, social media and cell phones, people today are bombarded with more targeted messages than at any other time in history!

Wherever the lies had come from, I knew I was hungry for the truth, and I believe most people are…at least the people who want to grow.

The Truth can be difficult and uncomfortable. The Truth can reveal things we do not want to admit or address. The Truth can hurt. That is why the World didn't want to meet the naked Truth.

Lies can be easier. They conceal things and help avoid confrontation. Think about a young boy who spills a drink and immediately lies about it. If he is let off the hook, he learns *not* to accept responsibility for his actions. If his parents make him admit what he did, it's harder, but he learns to be truthful and own his actions.

Unfortunately, lies don't help people heal and don't help people grow.

I will respect you enough to tell you the truth. I care about you enough to tell you the truth. I want you to grow, heal, mature, live a life you are proud of and have an amazingly positive impact on those around you. You can't do that if you're living and believing lies.

The title of every chapter in this book is a common lie. Each chapter then debunks the lie. You probably won't agree with some of these lies. That's okay, but I challenge you to read each chapter with an open mind, question your preconceived ideas and weigh the arguments as fairly as possible.

The truth is often uncomfortable, stretching, inconvenient, hurtful or otherwise hard to swallow. The truth is also necessary for you to reach your greatest potential. Don't let deception hold you back. You've been lied to, but you CAN handle the truth.

"Truth by definition is exclusive. If truth were all-inclusive, nothing would be false."

- Walter Martin

Chapter 1
Know *your* truth.

At the height of the Roman empire, Rome controlled roughly 50 separate provinces, each with its own governor who was the highest judicial authority, chief administrator, and ultimate military commander. Oversight was limited. Roman governors had a license to kill and would use capital punishment when they saw fit, regularly torturing, executing and hanging criminals on posts outside the city gates as examples to maintain order in their conquered lands.

In the province of Judaea, pilgrims flocked to the capital city for the week-long holiday celebration. The profitable revenue received during this time was surely appreciated by the governor. However, the tension among the locals, particularly the religious elite and others of influence, was palpable. Concern was growing more alarming by the hour. The city was in a fervor unlike any seen before.

In this fragile atmosphere at the crack of dawn, the local leaders dragged an accused man to the steps of the governor's palace, requesting, or rather demanding, his execution. This "criminal" wasn't like any other the governor had examined. He was mild-mannered, soft spoken, quiet, and seemingly reluctant to defend himself. Having an unsettling dream about this man, the governor's wife even came to him with a plea for his release.

During the governor's cross-examination, the accused spoke of his purpose and of truth, to which the governor responded with the most simple, yet most profound question man has ever asked.

"What is truth?"

And with those words lingering in the air, the governor walked out and back to the hostile crowd in an attempt to settle the matter as judiciously, or shrewdly, as possible.

That three word question asked centuries long ago is still unclear for many today.

"What is truth?"

Philosophers have spent thousands of years debating truth. There is no singular, universally agreed upon definition of truth, but respected philosophers throughout history as a whole have come up with logical, reasoned and rational understandings of truth that have stood the test of time.

For starters, truth is objective. It stands alone. Whether or not a person agrees or disagrees, a truth still exists. For instance, my son might tell me he did all his work to pass his classes in high school. If, however, he didn't complete all his courses and his school didn't give him credit for those courses, then what he told me is irrelevant. The truth would have been that he didn't pass his high school classes. Someone declaring something true or false has no bearing on the reality of the truth. Truth is true regardless of what one might claim.

Next, as Aristotle explained, the law of noncontradiction means that two contradicting theories can't both simultaneously be true. If two plus two is four, then two plus two can't also be five. It can't be raining and not be raining at the same time in the same place. If the sky is blue on a cloudless afternoon, it can't also not be blue. If your dog is alive, it can't also not be alive.

There is also a correspondence of truth theory which means that truth should reflect reality. Reality is how the world actually exists, as opposed to how some might imagine it. Some people have irrational fears. Others have irrational hopes and beliefs. Some people have perceptions that don't align with reality. If two people are in a disagreement, one way to help determine reality is by verifying one's position with reliable outside sources. When there is a car accident, and the two drivers have conflicting accounts of who is to blame, looking at skid marks, aligning the point of impact, hearing from other witnesses and reviewing video camera footage are ways to verify the reality of what happened.

Finally, truth is exclusive. Not everything can be true. If everything were true, then the word *truth* would have no meaning. It would be without purpose. However, since there are things that are not true, then the word *truth* holds value because it describes only those things that are true. It helps differentiate between lies and truth.

As in the legend about the Lie and the Truth, people in modern society are unfortunately becoming increasingly disinterested, or even offended, by the truth. To recognize the fact that truth is exclusive means that people who hold a different opinion would be wrong. This might hurt their feelings. And since we don't want to hurt their feelings, our society would rather accept a lie.

This is the train of thought, the logic, our society wants us to believe...to which I say, "That's just plain dumb!"

For fear of offending someone, people in our society act like truth should be subjective, contradicting and inclusive. Would you prefer to be inoffensive and wrong or risk being offensive but also being able to point someone in the right direction, the direction of truth.

Think about it personally. Would you rather live in ignorance and lies or would you prefer someone love you enough to tell you the truth when you've gone astray?

Let's role play for a minute. If your sister loses her job, falls into a minor depression and quits paying on her house but thinks it's all going to be okay, will you just let her house foreclosed on and lose $100,000 equity in her home? Or will you step in and tell her she either has to get a job or sell the house to save her $100,000? If her truth is that her house is gonna be okay, but the bank and court have a truth that her delinquency has reached the point of foreclosure and the property is now the bank's, can those two positions both be true?

No.

Should you let your sister live in her false truth?

No, at least not if you like her!

Now that we've established that truth is objective, doesn't contradict itself, reflects reality, is exclusive and that at certain times, we have a duty to share it, let's consider the current mantra: *know your truth* (or *live your truth*).

The problem with this trendy tagline is subtle, but that's also what makes this lie so dangerous. At first impression, this statement seems encouraging and even empowering. To know *your* truth, means that someone else can have *his* truth, a different truth. Basically, we can all have our own truths, and what is true for one doesn't have to be true

4

for another. So you can have your truth over there, and I'll have mine over here.

Unfortunately, that's not reality. If you have your truth, and another guy has his truth that contradicts your truth, they both can't be true.

For example, let's say Gabriela is married to John, and Gabriela believes that marriage should be monogamous for the life of the marriage. John, after a couple years of marriage, now believes that a monogamous relationship for the rest of his life is dull and holding him prisoner, so he should discreetly satisfy his belief as he sees fit. John wants to have affairs and one night stands outside his marriage. Gabriela and John have two conflicting truths; therefore, they both can't be true.

Another simple example is the ownership (property or land). A senior citizen might have saved a comfortable retirement after working for 50 years, but an opportunistic scammer might deceive them into sharing their account information and draining their savings. Two people might hold a different view on who rightfully owns a company, vehicle or other possessions. Two countries might both claim the same land. In these and millions of other situations, both parties can't *know their own truth*.

The sentiment to *know your truth* seems good enough at first. However, using the word *truth* in this context, misrepresents and devalues the concept of truth.

Truth is a loaded word. Truth is a positive word. Truth has great worth.

If one feels the need to communicate the sentiment of owning their future and being themselves, that's wonderful! But you have to change the terminology.

"Know your values."

"Follow your own way."

"Live your best life."

"Write your own story."

"YOU control your future."

Any of these will do, but people desperately want to throw the word *truth* in there, because it is such a powerful word. The *truth* packs a bigger punch. However, that's also why you can't just throw the word around. Truth is so powerful only because it's so rigid, resolute, realistic and exclusive.

Some people try to argue that there is no truth. These arguments usually don't last long. Eventually, someone in the conversation is smart enough to realize that saying that there is no truth is a self-defeating statement. If indeed there is no truth, then the statement, "There is no truth," can't be true...

In this sense, truth actually fights for itself.

Summary

Don't believe the lie that people can know, live and have their own truths. Truth is not subjective. It doesn't change from person to person. Truth is not your perception, or anyone else's for that matter. Truth is what's real. Two different people can't have their own truths if they are in conflict with each other. If this offends you, I don't apologize. I care about you enough to tell you the truth, just like a loving parent cares for his child. A child might want to play in the street, eat ice cream all day, and watch endless hours of Youtube, but good parents love their children enough not to allow those things to become their reality or their "truth." The truth is that there is right and wrong in this world. We don't get to choose and decide what our truth is. We get to choose our clothes for the day, what food we put in our mouths, who we hang out with, where we go, what colors we favor, what we value and thousands of other decisions. We don't get to choose our truth. Don't lie to yourself, pretending you can make up your own truth. Truth exists outside of any person. It is objective. It doesn't bend to the whims of man. It is powerful. May this book help you discover more truth.

"You are more than the choices that you've made,
   You are more than the sum of your past mistakes,
You are more than the problems you create,
   You've been remade."[1]

– Tenth Avenue North

Chapter 2
You're worthless.

"But you, cursed from birth," Mr. Mendez scowled condescendingly as he looked harshly into Will's eyes. "A man who God Himself turned his back on!"[2]

For Will, this insult tore deeper than the other thousands he had received in his life. Not because of *what* was said, but because of *who* said it. Mr. Mendez, who was both his employer and the ringmaster of an inspirational circus, was also supposed to be Will's friend now, or so he thought.

Previously, Will was a freak in a carnival sideshow. He wasn't just a normal freak though. Will was the freak of the freaks. The conjoined twins were before him, as was the bearded lady and the tattooed man. You always save the best, or in this case, the worst–the most hideous–for last. With no arms or legs, Will was literally a stub of a man.

It wasn't like he had nubs for arms or legs.

Nope.

Worse.

Only torso and foot.

Will thought he had finally found his place in life. He was now with the Butterfly Circus, and he hadn't faced the taunts and jeers for some time. He assumed his colleagues were friends also, but now his closest friend, so he thought, was mocking him like all the others.

With pain in his voice as he fought back the tears in his eyes, Will demanded to know why he would say that.

"Because you believe it," Mr. Mendez responded, and then with tenderness in his voice, "but if you could only see the beauty that can come from ashes."[2]

So many young people believe the lie that they are worthless.

You are not worthless.

Say it out loud.

"I am not worthless."

Say it again.

"I am not worthless."

Say it with conviction.

"I am NOT worthless."

If you can't say it, or if you're having a hard time saying it, then unfortunately, somewhere along the line, you have already bought into the lie. It's time you start speaking life into yourself. Speak the truth over yourself that you have worth. It also might be time you start surrounding yourself with more positive people.

I don't know your background. I don't know if you've been neglected or abused. I don't know if you were a prostitute, alcoholic, porn addict or drug dealer. I don't know if you've abused others. I don't know if you failed in school, dropped out of school or can't read.

But what I know is this: that you have worth. I truly believe that. I believe you are valuable. I believe it for two reasons.

The first is that I heard someone once say that people were made in the image of God; therefore, all people have value. That hit differently. It was wonderful and freeing at the same time. It made sense.

My second reason that you have value is pretty simple. No one else on the planet has lived your story. Only you can share your story how it should be told.

Maybe you have heard, "We are better together," or "Diversity makes us stronger." However you understand this concept, it is true. Only you can fully and completely share your story. It is intricate and nuanced, and only you lived it. You contribute a piece to humanity that no one else can add.

I know you've made mistakes. I have too. We all have. And yes, some of us have done things much worse than others. But that is not who you have to be. It might be who you were, but you can change who you are.

Clive Staples Lewis shared the sobering realization that, "You can't go back and change the beginning, but you can start where you are and change the ending."

The remaining chapters of your life have not yet been written. If you have done horrible things, make amends the best you can and move forward doing good. If you need to apologize to someone, do it. If you need to cut certain vices, toxic people or negative influences out of your life, do it. Start the process of changing yourself–improving yourself. If there's something in your life that you think you can't forgive yourself for, start learning how to forgive yourself. And you start that by setting a boundary not to allow yourself to do that again. (And if it happens, set the boundary again…sometimes, it takes time.)

You have potential to make a positive difference in the world, starting today. Sure, we have potential for negative impact, and all of us have spread some of that. But we all have made positive choices at times. Whether you helped your mom or neighbor get a chore done, helped pick up something your friend dropped, shared a kind smile, stood up for someone being picked or something else, YOU have helped someone else at some point in your life. You are capable of making a positive impact. You have that power. I challenge you to do one positive thing today. And tomorrow.

The story I shared about Will at the beginning was not a true story (the true story is much worse in many ways). It is from the short film, *The Butterfly Circus*.

But did you catch what Mr. Mendez said? Let me summarize it in three words.

"Beauty from ashes."

Many people are quick to reach the conclusion that their life is in shambles or ashes. And it may be. But that does not have to be the end. You can make something beautiful out of the ashes.

Years ago, I had the privilege of seeing Nick Vujicic, the actor who plays *Will* in *The Butterfly Circus*, at a conference, and it was one of the most motivational speeches I've ever heard. More recently, I watched his Ted Talk on YouTube, and it was pretty good too. It only had like 8 million views!

Can you imagine being born without arms or legs? How would you get around? How would you eat? Drink? Use the restroom? Scratch an itch? Date? Answer the phone? Make a call? How would you feel

12

about yourself? How would you feel as a young boy when all the kids made fun of you?

That was Nick's life. He felt so worthless that he tried to drown himself when he was young. If he had succeeded, the world would be a much darker place.

Nick overcame that lie. He found God at age 15. He began to believe that he had worth, largely because his parents spoke positively about him on a regular basis.

According to his website, "Nick has traveled to 78 countries, presenting on 3500 stages, to crowds as large as 800,000 people."[3]

After you finish reading this book, I recommend you pick up Nick's bestselling *Life without Limits: Inspiration for a Ridiculously Good Life.*[4]

I know that my life has been blessed because Nick refused to believe the lie that he was worthless.

Don't you believe that lie either.

Summary

I heard the late Dr. Cliff Schimmels, professor and author, speak at Lee University years ago, and he shared about a Sunday school class he was in as a young child. Sometimes, they would color. There was a cigar box of crayons, and most of the kids would run up and grab the best and brightest crayons first. However, there was a little girl that would sheepishly go up after the other kids, get a few of the broken, dirty crayons, and return to her seat. The teacher would show off all the pictures, and that little, shy girl routinely colored the most beautiful pictures with those broken crayons.

Start to color. You have worth. You are valuable. Believe in yourself. Speak some positive truth into your life and the lives of others. Show the world what a beautiful picture you can color with the broken crayons of your life.

"I took my darkness and turned it into light for someone."

— Mary J. Blige

Chapter 3
You can't.

Some *jerk* told Mary, "You can't."

Mary had been in a tough place. Life hadn't always been great for her. There was darkness. Even talking about it now, years later in an interview, the emotions were evident on her face and in her voice. Hurt. Disappointment. Anger. Frustration.[1]

However, at some point in her life Mary learned that the jerk lied to her. He had told her that she couldn't, but in March of 2023, the children's book *Mary Can!* was released to inspire kids to believe that they *can* indeed.

Mary is the author.

Not only is she now an inspirational, successful author, but according to Wikipedia, Mary J. Blige has been nominated for over 200 awards and won 88 of those awards including Grammy Awards, Billboard Awards, an Emmy, BET Awards and a plethora of others.[2] Just one of these major accomplishments is more than most of us ever achieve. Look at the number again.

Eighty-eight!

Eighty-eight big time awards. Talk about impressive. Talk about proving the haters wrong. If Mary J. Blige never wins anything else, she will be one of the most accomplished individuals in the entertainment business–ever. But she's still going strong. She's still doing the things she *can* do: the things others told her she can't.

Has anyone told you that you can't do something?

I'm not talking about piddly things, like bottle flipping, or superficial things like becoming a billionaire investing in cryptocurrency. I'm talking about your dreams. What do you feel that you were made to do? What are you passionate about? What brings you joy, peace and fulfillment? What do you love? Do you love to dance? Do you love to write? Do you love to code? Do you want to help children in the foster care system? Do you have a dream to be a fighter pilot? Is your dream to have a loving spouse, peacefully raising a family in the suburbs? (Might sound simple but is actually much more challenging than you'd imagine.) Do you want to climb Mt. Kilimanjaro? Do you want to spend your life hiking with someone you love? Do you want to be an inventor, brain surgeon, politician or youtuber (five years ago, this last one was a joke, but not anymore)?

Let me ask you a question. Can you do it?

Has someone told you that, "You can't"? Sometimes, people don't tell us that we can't, but they ask questions or make statements creating self doubt in us.

People might subtly say, "Wow! That sounds crazy. I would never even try."

The negative Nancy in your life will be more emphatic: "That's just impossible these days."

Jealous people will question your motives, ability and character.

Even your own friends and family will ask questions and make statements about whether it's something you can or cannot do.

16

As a side note here, let me point out that no family or friendship is perfect. Hopefully, your family loves you and is asking you questions out of care and concern. These conversations can be tough, but they are beneficial. There are also friends and family that are not healthy and won't always have your best interests in mind. Some conversations are born out of hurt, jealousy, fear, arrogance, pessimism and other negative emotions and feelings. Use wisdom and discernment in knowing which conversations are productive and worth continuing and which ones you need to disregard.

For example, let me share two separate conversations in which one of my inner circle people challenged me on whether or not I could do something I was dreaming to do.

The first was when I had started to write a book a decade or so ago. It was going to be a short book (100-130 pages). I had the title and description of every chapter, the introduction and the first chapter completed. Then the person I cared about the most challenged me by saying that having a far greater knowledge in this area, this person did not feel that s/he could even write a book on the subject, suggesting much less how could I?

This person didn't come right out and say, "Matt, you can't do it," but that is basically what was communicated. I never finished that book. I'm not sure I ever completed another chapter after that conversation.

But I don't blame that person. I was insecure. At that point in my life, I allowed what others thought and their perception of me to carry more weight than it should have. I was not yet as strong mentally or emotionally as I needed to be. That book was never completed, and I accept full responsibility for it. I am not a victim. Others don't (or at

17

least should not be able to) control my life by their words. At the end of the day, I am an adult, and I make my own decisions. I myself made the choice at that time not to pursue that dream.

Another conversation I had was a few years later and with another person extremely close to me–my mom.

My mom is a great mother. She loves her family and has made sacrifices her entire life so that others can be happy and successful. I love her dearly, but she was not happy when I told her about my plans to go to Botswana to serve at Love Botswana Outreach Mission…and take her only three grandchildren with me.

Like I said, my mom loves me. However, she had asked multiple times if I was sure that this was the right thing, had I thought about all the challenges, had I thought about the kids adjusting, if this was the right timing and so on.

Again, the words, "You can't do this," weren't said verbatim or emphatically, but they seemed to have been implied. Or at least, I inferred them.

I also had to make a decision. Would I back out of the plan to go serve in Maun, Botswana, or would I stay the course that I felt was right for me?

At this point in my life, I was a bit more mature and had a little more wisdom. I had a conviction that going was the right thing to do, and we went.

So what was different when it came to these two "dream" decisions in my life? Why had one dream died and the other thrived?

Well, first, I was different. Like I said, I had grown. However, there was another major difference, and that was the *motive* of the person challenging me in whether or not I could actually do it. In the

18

conversation about Botswana, the motive was in the best interest of me and my family, specifically of my children. I respected the source of this motive and listened, prayerfully weighing the options.

On the other hand, the motive behind the challenge I received about writing that other book did not have my best interest in mind. There was definitely negative opposition that I would have had to push through. At that time, I chose the path of least resistance. I had received the message that I can't do that, and I didn't.

Looking back, I wonder how it would have played out and where I'd be now in life. It was not a major life long dream or anything. But it was something I was passionate about for a few years. Part of me wishes I had followed that dream. Another part of me recognizes how much I have grown since then, how good my life is now and is at peace with the growing pains. After all, pain is a great teacher and helps build strength, resilience and perseverance.

Stephen King was rejected dozens of times before finally receiving his first publishing deal. Oprah was fired from her television anchor position, having been referred to as "unfit" for TV. Sylvester Stallone is said to have been rejected 1,500 times!

What if Stephen King, Oprah or Sly had listened to those people who told them that they "can't"? The world would be short of over 30 NY Times best sellers. The most watched talk show which played in over 100 countries would never have happened. Film fans would have missed out on the *Rocky*, the *Rambo* and the *Expendables* series as well as Stallone's roles in about 70 other films. And not to forget, hundreds of average people would not have received their free cars from Oprah.

What about you? Is there anything you have a passion for that you have chosen to avoid chasing because someone told you that you can't?

The world just might be a brighter place if you believe in yourself instead of believing that lie.

Summary

There will always be doubters, haters and negative people challenging what they think you can or can't do. Be careful who you listen to. Words have power, but they only have as much power as you give them. If you have a good, honest dream, don't let some bum ruin it for you. *A Million Miles Away* tells the story of a migrant farm worker who overcame years of prejudice and 11 official rejections before finally becoming a NASA astronaut![3] The original David and Goliath story recounts how the sitting king told David he could *not* fight the giant because David was too small, but David had a different perspective on his physical body, writing, "I am fearfully and wonderfully made."[4] We all know what David did to Goliath. Who or what are the giants in your life that have told you that you can't do something? They are lying. You can!

"Be careful what you wish for
'Cause you just might get it all
You just might get it all
And then some you don't want"

— Chris Daughtry

Chapter 4
You deserve a nice meal.

It goes something like this. You're busy. You have a job. You also have to go to class. You have homework from that class.You might be a full time student with a part time job, or you might work full time and be a part time student. You might be out of school and desperately looking for a job to pay the bills. Or you might just be working to make ends meet. Wherever you are, it is *not* easy.

You don't have much money to spare. You're not broke, but you're definitely not comfortable. And even though you know you shouldn't be spending extra money because you'll probably have to pay your cell phone bill with a credit card again, at least once a week–rather more like three or four times a week–you find yourself at a restaurant or ordering DoorDash.

Then, you don't even enjoy it that much. You have this cloud of guilt hanging over your head. You mention it to one of your good friends who responds, "It's okay. You're working hard. You're a good person. You deserve a nice meal."

BOOM, there it is.

Of course your friend is going to tell you that you deserve it. He cares about you. He knows you're stressed. He knows you're a good person, and he wants to relieve your stress.

Since before Y2K (if you don't know what that is, google it), I've been eating out so I have some perspective and experience.

I've personally known hundreds of people in this exact scenario or one similar to it. There was a time in my life that it was me too. If this happens once a month or so, no big deal. In fact, there is nothing wrong with eating out when you can afford it.

But reality is different. Many people spend more money eating out than they do eating at home. Many people eat lunch out regularly. And plenty of people enjoy frappuccino, lattes, smoothies, energy drinks, and other fancy ways to hydrate.

You can actually eat a full well-rounded dinner at home for less than the price of a cup of coffee or boba tea at most places. Seriously. I've regularly bought chicken or steak at the grocery store, come home, cooked it and paired it with a salad and potato. My wife and I both ate until we were full, all for less than $12. Less than 10 bucks if it was on sale. (I love a bargain!) That's a nice full meal for the cost of $5-6 each! Most lattes cost more than that, before the tip…which it seems as if society is demanding at least a 20% tip for pouring some liquid into a styrofoam cup these days, but that's another story.

That same meal at a restaurant for the two of us after tax and tip is easily $40-$50 on the low end. In that scenario, you are literally spending 400% more on a meal. Even if you're trying to nitpick my numbers, if I'm half wrong, you're still paying 200% (three times) more for your meal.

Any way you slice it, the point is you are harming yourself.

22

How? It's plain and simple; think about it. You are jeopardizing your financial future, and you know it. And you're lying to yourself telling yourself that it's ok. You even tell your friend how you're feeling in hopes of getting his affirmation. The stress is growing because you know you're in a worse spot for excess spending when you were already tight. The guilt is growing. Every time you do this, you are a step closer to creating a long term bad habit or giving the habit that much more power and control over you.

Yes, you are feeding that habit of instant gratification, even when it's harmful.

Ouch! Did I hit a nerve? I hope so. Why? Because I care about you. I might even care about you more than that friend. I'm not saying he is a bad dude. Your friends should care about you.

But there are different levels of friendship. I've known a lot of folks over the years. At different points, I've called many of them friends. But most were not *real* friends. Most of them cared about me…but not enough to look me in the eye and kindly, but firmly, tell me something I didn't want to hear. Those friends are rare. Hold on to those friends.

A lot of people are just going to placate you. And that's fine. It's even polite.

But if you listen carefully to your conscience, you know.

You and I may never be friends in a practical sense, but I will be your friend enough to tell you the truth. And the truth is (unless you are wealthy) quit telling yourself you deserve a nice meal multiple times a week. And quit listening to people tell you the same thing when it comes to being irresponsible with money.

I'll do the math for you. If you spend an extra $50 eating out a week (as opposed to what you would have spent eating at home), that's over $2,500 a year. If you make $25,000, you literally chose to spend 10% of your income on something you didn't need.

No wonder, Americans spent nearly $1.5 trillion dollars on food away from home in 2024[2]. In fact, according to the U.S. Department of Agriculture, "Food-away-from-home spending accounted for 55 percent of total food expenditures."[2] That's right, Americans now spend the *majority* of their food budget on eating out. It's not just you. It's a trend.

Now, I'm not against eating out, but I am against eating out to the point that it becomes harmful to you and your future. Reconsider that 55 percent statistic. Marinate on it. Does it make financial sense or even common sense for Americans to spend the majority of their food budget on eating out? What is a healthy percent? Ten percent? I can even see twenty percent. But when people spend $550 of a $1,000 food budget on a service, they have a problem. And not just a financial problem, they might have a self-control problem. Almost no financial advisor or life coach will sit down with you to discuss your budget and propose spending the majority of your food money on eating out...yet, that's the reality of life in the U.S.

Why? Because we want what we want. We want it now. And we'll pay for it, even if it's not what's best for us. It's easy, and it's convenient.

It's harder to fix food at home. Someone might have to sit down once a week, make a grocery list, go shopping, prepare the meal and clean the dishes. Of course, some people might just use AI to see what meal they can make from a few ingredients they have in the

24

house. (Please don't mention Instacart, unless you can mathematically prove the cost you're paying for the delivery is made up by you working that extra hour.)

Single moms have it the hardest. Often they are paid the least with the greatest number of responsibilities. Young people starting out often don't have a fully stocked kitchen. Some apartments might not have all the appliances. You might not have a convenient grocery store nearby. It won't be easy...but then again, nothing worthwhile really is.

Look at it this way. Eating out regularly is preventing you from adequately paying *your* bills and saving and investing your money in a way that is best for you and your goals. In fact, you are actively paying *someone else's* bills and contributing to their finances.

Unsuccessful people make decisions based on what is easy and convenient. Mature, responsible people make decisions based on what is best. Broke people spend when they can't afford it. Successful people say, "No," now, so they can say, "Yes," later.

Let me tell you about a former coworker of mine. I picked up a summer job selling fireworks after my divorce, and Josh (not his real name) kinda taught me the ropes in the stockroom. It's not a typical job for a teacher, but I did it for a few reasons. First, the extra money helped pay for vacation for a single dad with three kids that summer. Also, I desperately needed something to keep me busy on the days I didn't have my kids. Of course, I got a nice discount on the fireworks to feed my inner pyro. The people were great, and we had a blast (dad joke intended, if you wish)!

Josh and I would chat about life quite a bit. He was a hard worker. Not only was Josh a father like me, he had a former life that seemed like everything was together before his family split in a divorce. We were both kind of finding ourselves again.

Josh would help stock fireworks a few days each week after he finished his other jobs. He drove a local truck making deliveries. Then, he'd cut grass for a few hours. Then, he'd come in for a short shift to stock fireworks with a Red Bull in his hand. He worked nearly every day including weekends. Because he was way too busy to eat a decent lunch, he'd drop around 10 bucks on fast food and/or snacks from the gas station for lunch every day (this was back when prices on everything were much cheaper).

Schedules at the store were somewhat flexible, and Josh had been there for a number of seasons, so he could pretty much come and work as he pleased. However, I noticed he often only worked two to four hour shifts. Now, we weren't making gobs of money. In fact, we weren't making a whole lot more than minimum wage (maybe a couple bucks more).

I asked him about the daily Red Bulls, and he responded that it was the only way he could make it through the day. Apparently, they had cost a few dollars each, but most gas stations sold them 2 for $5 making them more affordable.

As I thought about it, I realized that Josh spent at least $5 every single time he worked a shift at the fireworks store and often more because sometimes he'd buy snacks at the gas station. Most of his shifts ended up only being two to five hours. Being a bit of a nerd, I kept running the numbers in my head. Then it dawned on me, and I realized that these short shifts, after taxes, energy drinks and often snacks meant he was probably only netting about $8-$25 per shift! Yes, that's correct.

I tried to gently talk to him about it, but he was convinced he had to work as much as possible to make money to provide for him and his kid. The money spent on energy drinks and grabbing grub on the go didn't phase him because it was a way of life. He was a hard worker and he deserved it. What was the alternative?

Well for starters, he could have quit his fireworks job. Then he wouldn't need the extra energy drinks and snacks. And with the extra 15-20 hours a week, he could have spent more time with his kid, getting some rest and shopping for groceries for his lunches and snacks during the week, which by the way would probably have saved him the money he was working so hard for at the third job anyway.

And how would this have affected Josh's life overall? First of all, his stress level would have dropped. His physical health would be much improved by eating less sugars, artificial sweeteners and junk food. With the extra time, his relationships with his kid, family and friends would have the opportunity to grow stronger and improve. And the extra time and rest would likely help him to think more clearly, plan better and have more peace of mind.

But, life is busy. Life is hard. Josh deserved a nice meal and a Red Bull. And so do you, right?

Or do you?

I don't think you do.

In fact, I think you deserve more. I think you deserve to learn self-control. I think you deserve to live your life so you can respect yourself and don't have to carry extra guilt. I think you deserve to mature to the point where you can plan, shop, cook a few decent meals and clean the dishes. That's right you deserve to be independent. And you deserve the couple extra hundred bucks each month that you will have to put toward your goals (and not your mouth). With the extra money, you can pay off debt, save for a downpayment on a house, save for vacation, invest, help others or do something else that you feel will be best for you and your family if you're at that stage of life.

Or you can eat it. It's your choice.

Summary

As Americans, many of us have a way of satisfying our desires by telling ourselves, and getting others to tell us, that we "deserve it." We tell ourselves the following:

"I deserve a nice vacation because this past year was tough."

"I deserve to go to an expensive college" (often in spite of a lack of effort in school and low grades).

"I deserve a $50,000 wedding because I'm only getting married once."

"I deserve not to have to work at all while in college, so I can focus on my studies," (Rabbit trail: research indicates working part time results in higher grades than not working at all.)[3]

"Even though I'm in debt and struggling to pay my bills, I deserve a nice meal because I'm working hard."

Eating out at a nice restaurant, going to exotic places, throwing an expensive wedding and other luxuries are not in of themselves bad. In fact, they can be positive and wonderful under the right circumstances. The problem is when people lie to themselves and pay too high a price *now* for something they can better afford and appreciate *later*. Often when people satiate their desires now, the price tag comes with guilt, regret, debt, delaying goals or a mixture of these.

Nothing is as frustrating as going on a vacation and not being able to enjoy it because you put it on a credit card and can't shake the dread of wondering how many months or years it will take to pay it off.

Start telling yourself the truth: you deserve to wait now so you can meet your goals and fully appreciate your fancy meals, nice car and other luxuries without regret later.

"October: This is one of the particularly dangerous months to invest in stocks. Other dangerous months are July, January, September, April, November, May, March, June, December, August, and February."

— Mark Twain

"The safest way to double your money is to fold it over and put it in your pocket."

— Kin Hubbard

Chapter 5
OPM is the secret to getting rich.

"You shouldn't have done that," she said to me matter-of-factly. Well, she's more of an acquaintance, specifically, a family member of a family member.

Regardless, I was taken aback. My wife and I put 20% down on our house, which also has a very low interest rate. This came up in our conversation as this lady has a job that relates to interest rates. She went on to explain how we could have put a minimal down payment or no down payment (insert eyeroll emoji here), invested the rest and would have been better off.

"At such a low interest rate, it's like free money!" she said with a laugh.

This sounds fresh. It sounds exciting. Mathematically, It sounds like it should work. It seems savvy, even sexy. Maybe we should have done just that, so we can use that extra money every year?

But one specific thing, and not a minor thing, made the whole conversation feel a little off...the lady giving us this advice is in a worse financial position than us! In fact, she'd likely jump at the opportunity to swap financial positions with me and my wife.

For those of you who don't know, OPM is slang for Other People's Money. The concept is basically borrowing money, then investing it to earn a higher return while repaying the lower payments and keeping the difference.

Supporters of the OPM movement throw out words like "leverage," "capital," "investment portfolio" and other financially sounding gibberish to describe the process. Sometimes, it can be very confusing. Other times, it can seem logical and legit. The more they talk, the more you can see yourself with a margarita in hand while sunbathing on sandy, white beaches in the Caribbean awaiting your massage. There's a supermodel in a bikini or Fabio with his shirt off walking up the beach as the wind blows through his hair...

WAKE UP!!!

Come back to reality.

I heard a long time ago that if something sounds too good to be true, it probably is. For the vast majority of people, OPM is going to bring more damage to your financial future than wealth.

For starters, champions of OPM hardly ever mention the risks. There are virtually no investments that *guarantee* a return that is significantly higher than the rate at which you can borrow money long term; therefore, you have a risk of losing your money.

In my case, the mortgage on my house was around three percent. If the amount I invested instead of paying down my mortgage was $50,000, then I'm immediately starting $1,500 in the hole each year. In other words, I would have to earn greater than $1,500 on my investment every year to make a profit on the extra mortgage interest I'm paying by not using the money on a downpayment.

But for the sake of argument, let's say I withheld my downpayment and invested it elsewhere. I could have invested the money in one of these typical investments: CD's, stocks, mutual funds or put it as a down payment on a rental house. The CD's wouldn't return much significantly higher than the 3% on my mortgage. Stocks are extremely risky and volatile. A mutual fund is less risky than single stocks but still more risky than most are comfortable with if they will need the money back in less than a few years. The return on real estate seems to have the highest potential return; however, it is an understood principle of investing that the higher the expected return, the higher the risk.

What could have gone right? I could have picked good stocks at lower prices, waited until they went up and sold them at higher prices. This practice is actually referred to as "timing the market," and is great in theory but is notorious for being impossible to do.

The mutual fund is similar in performance but with less volatility.

I could have bought a rental house, hopefully at the right price. It could have had no hidden issues. I could have gotten good renters that paid their rent on time and didn't do serious damage to the property.

What could have gone wrong? Obviously, the stocks or mutual funds could have gone down. Even if the stock or fund portfolio stayed relatively even, the $1,500 saved in interest would have been lost. There could have been hidden structural, electrical, plumbing or other significant issues in the house. The renters might have destroyed the place, or it might have taken a number of months to get renters. Also, we recently had this little thing called COVID, during which defaulted renters were allowed to stay without being evicted for an extended period of time.

Am I saying never to take risks? No. People take risks all the time. There's a risk of getting into a fatal car crash when driving to the store, but it is an extremely minimal risk. Most people willingly accept this risk. What I am saying is that it is in your best interest to *minimize* the risks you take, and often when people use OPM, they are unnecessarily increasing their risks and ignoring other factors and benefits to consider when it comes to OPM.

What other factors should you consider?

First of all, when many people borrow money, they lose peace of mind. For some, it's a little peace of mind, and for others, it could be so much peace of mind that they begin losing sleep. People in debt have more of a tendency to worry. I don't have a scientific study at my fingertips, but who do you think sleep better: people with debt or people who own all their assets?

Also, all investments require time and energy. Certain investments require significantly more time, energy, frustration and hassle than others.

Buying stocks or mutual funds requires time and effort. For some this is a lot of time, and for others, less. However, even those who are inclined mathematically still must put in a few hours of research on the front end, then either set up a personal account or meet with a broker, then do more research to time your sell and more time transferring the funds in time to make on-time payments on the money you borrowed, etc.

I am not suggesting never to invest in the stock market. There is potential for large gains and ways to minimize risk. If you are investing your own money with confidence and knowledge and have time (like a few years or longer) to decrease the risk of down years, you might be in a good and healthy position to invest in the market. On the other hand, when using OPM, there is a date of when the money must be paid back and if payments are missed, fees can be added, interest rates can be raised, notes can be called, etc. This is increased risk.

A rental home requires even more time and energy, especially at the beginning, and even later in between renters. You have to research homes, usually work with a realtor, have an inspection(s), create a rental agreement, interview and review potential tenants, collect rent each month, fix anything that goes wrong with the property, etc. Or you can go the Airbnb route, which from what I've gathered either requires that much more time cleaning and communicating or more money paying someone to do this for you.

You have to ask yourself, "Is the expected return on my investment more than the time and energy I am putting in?"

There is a similar question to ask, "Is the return worth the time and energy I am having to take from other things (like family)?"

You also need to consider if there are any unseen advantages you are missing by not using OPM. In the example of my down payment, I was able to avoid paying PMI, private mortgage insurance, which would have been around $140 a month (nearly $1,700 annually). If we would need to sell and the market slows, we'll definitely have enough equity to have that flexibility. (I've known multiple people whose homes sat on the market for months while they continued paying a mortgage on an empty house after they had moved.) Also, we were able to get a better rate because we were able to afford a 15 year mortgage. Had we wanted to have more cash available now, we could have opted for the 30 year mortgage to have a smaller monthly payment.

Finally, like my mom always said, "You can't have your cake and eat it too."

I think this is one of the dumbest sayings (sorry, mom), but nothing is more appropriate to refer to OPM. You can't both be using money on personal stuff and investing it simultaneously. You can't be earning money in the stock market and use that same money to pay your bills. Ideally, you could be using some from a rent payment, but there are a number of big "if"s that must work out correctly first. In order to benefit from OPM, you have to be a bit of a magician. First, you have to get the money from other people, then invest it, then get it back, then give it back to the other people that you borrowed it from, with interest might I add, and hope you made enough profit for it to be worth it.

While there are indeed some savvy people with plenty of extra time and energy to jump through all the right hoops at the right time and benefit from OPM, reality is much different for the large majority. I know, and you probably know, people who have had cars repossessed, houses foreclosed on, family members that don't talk anymore and co-signed loans that went into default all because of OPM. I do know one or two successes of OPM, but the ratio is staggeringly high compared to those who are harmed by OPM.

Whatever it is that makes people wealthy, one thing is clear. Using other people's money hasn't gotten many, many more people broke than rich.

On his radio program, best-selling author Dave Ramsey regularly says, "Your income is your greatest wealth-building tool."

I agree with that statement. I'd also suggest hard work, living within your means, saving for retirement early and making quality low risk long term investments has a lot to do with how wealthy you become.

My grandparents advised against debt. My grandfather was a WWII vet who retired from the post office. My grandma worked in the school cafeteria. They saved and invested 10% of everything they earned. They didn't leverage OPM. They bought some stock. I think they saved up and bought an orange grove once. They bought a lot of bonds (interest rates on bonds were much better several decades back). They paid off their house. They lived beneath their means, but enjoyed a very good life. In their 60s, they finally applied for a credit card, because someone told them they needed it. With a net worth of over a quarter million dollars about 30 years ago, they were denied the credit card. Go figure.

They didn't care. They didn't need it.

My grandparents lived the American dream. Their parents immigrated through Ellis Island and valued hard work. My grandparents worked hard. They saved their money. They invested their money, not other people's money. They vacationed at the beach every summer. They went out to eat. They visited relatives in Italy and hosted relatives from Italy here a couple times. They enjoyed life, family and friends. After my grandpa passed, my grandma eventually moved into an assisted living facility for a couple years and later a nursing home for a few more years. I don't know the exact figures, but they also left their children, grandchildren and great grandchildren a decent inheritance. While they were not "filthy rich," I think many people both American and foreign would have referred to them as "rich."

Speaking of being rich, maybe, there's more to life than money, like purpose, peace, joy, love, values and, for many, God.

Summary

I am not sure there is a secret to getting rich, but if there is, OPM is *not* it. In fact, for most people, OPM does significantly more harm than good. Finances are important. You need to manage them well. Maybe we should shift our mindset from buying and selling to stewarding. Americans as a whole are some of the wealthiest people in the world, yet 60% live paycheck to paycheck.[1] Why? For starters, it seems there is no end to the way we can spend our money. We are inundated with an endless stream of ads for services and junk we don't even need. Just like the viral quote, "We buy stuff we don't need with money we don't have to impress people we don't even like." Perhaps, we should stop striving to get more money quickly and start saving, investing and managing the money we do have better.

"The best time to plant a tree was 20 years ago. The next best time is today."

— Chinese Proverb

Chapter 6
At some point, you will have to grow up.

I'm sure you've heard this spoken a number of times, even if it wasn't spoken to you or if the phrasing was closer to, "Eventually, you gotta grow up." And when said in the right context, this can be true; however, it is most often spoken in a context that conveys the wrong message.

This can be true when said to young children. This can be true when spoken to middle schoolers about to go high school. This can even be true for teenagers about to enter adulthood.

However, the large majority of times I've heard, "Well, you're gonna have to grow at some point, Johnny," this statement actually communicated a false message and did more harm than good.

This phrase isn't typically said in a calm manner when having a productive conversation about entering the next phase of life with a young man or lady. It's most often spoken in frustration with boys, and sometimes girls, who are nowhere near the maturity level you'd expect.

It might be that I've heard this more than my fair share because I'm a middle school teacher; however, I've heard this out in public, at the ballpark and with friends and family plenty. And the person to which the comment is almost always directed is usually the least mature of the bunch.

The comment doesn't follow a single mistake a kid made. It comes out most often when an adult has reached their tipping point after consistent immature behavior.

You wouldn't say this to a four year old who lost his sock. He's four, and he's going to lose a sock. You wouldn't say this to an eight year old who forgot to do her homework once in the past couple months. That happens.

On the other hand, the 12 year old kid who keeps screaming obnoxiously for five minutes at the park is likely to receive this warning. Then, there's the young teenager who has multiple dirty dishes left in her room from the past three weeks and refuses to clean her room. There's the soon-to-be legal adult who complains about the price of college and not having money but is constantly playing video games, doesn't have a job and missed the FAFSA deadline to receive financial aid for college. These are the recipients of parents, friends and family's ire of "having to grow up *someday*."

But that sentiment is rather inaccurate. The truth is that these children–and I use that term deliberately–these *children* need to grow up *now*. They are actually past due to have grown up.

When immature people are told that they *will* need to grow up "at some point," they are given a false reality. They are hearing that they will need to get it together *in the future*. This allows them to continue poor habits. They are still feeling acceptance. Their behavior is being excused, and the people around them are contributing to their lack of progress and maturity. They are being enabled.

Yes, if you are a person who tells people who are obviously behaving lower than what you know their maturity level should be that they will *eventually* have to grow up, you are an *enabler*! You are doing them a disservice. You are essentially lying to them and permitting them to continue in their foolishness. You need to love them enough to tell them the truth. And the truth for many young people is that they need to grow up *now*.

The quote "Growing old is mandatory. Growing up is optional," has been attributed to Walt Disney. I concede that if Disney said this, he was likely trying to make the point that there are times when older people can still have the option to play like children. However, it also works the other way. Some people who have aged still act like children in ways that are foolish, unproductive and rather frustrating to others.

At times, immature behavior is fun. At times, it is acceptable. Even I love a cheesy dad joke or good prank as much as the next guy. However, there are times when that same immature behavior is a nuisance and annoying to others. At times, it can be borderline dangerous, and at other times, not only is it reckless, but it can have disastrous and even deadly consequences.

Two recent examples come to mind. Both cases involved young men and made national headlines in the summer of 2023.

In the first case, there were some high school seniors on a trip to the Bahamas. They went on an evening cruise. After dark on a dare, a young man jumped off the boat into the water. He was seen swimming on the surface briefly before he vanished. The search was called off seven days later. Unfortunately, he was never seen again. What started as a practical joke had a tragic end.

The other incident occurred on the other side of the globe. A man in the U.S. military was in South Korea, and seemingly ordered to return to the States. He managed to go on a tour of a Korean border village and crossed the line. As of this writing, the outcome is unknown but multiple media outlets have reported that he is in custody in N. Korea, typically a very dire situation for Americans. [Update during revision: he was released two months later and eventually pled guilty to five charges.][1]

Obviously, no one is perfect, and we have all made mistakes. Sometimes, there are no consequences at all, or they are minimal. But from a mathematical standpoint, the more often childlike or reckless behavior occurs, the chances of something severe happening increases.

If people have warned you that you will eventually need to grow up, I will gladly help you dispel that myth. You need to grow up now. And a real friend will tell you so.

After my divorce, I did something dumb. (Well, I've done a number of dumb things, but I'm thinking of one instance in particular.) I talked with a good friend of mine, and he said to call him if I found myself in that situation again. So a couple weeks later, the situation presented itself. I called him. We had a good chat.

Then, I ended up doing that same dumb thing again!

When I told him later, he just gave me that look and said, "Hey, if you're gonna reach out to me and then do whatever the heck you want anyway, then next time, don't call me. Don't waste my time."

Boom!

Cold.

Just like that.

It occurred to me that my immature behavior was jeopardizing a valued friendship of well over a decade. He didn't placate me. He didn't enable me. He didn't say, "Aw, I understand. You've been divorced, and you're hurt."

42

Nope.

He cared about me enough to let me know I needed to grow up now.

I have known another man for several years who is about 50 years old. I think he's quit more jobs in the past five years than I've had in almost 25 years of working. I've heard excuse after excuse after excuse about why every single job is not the right fit.

He has received the message in his life that he can grow up "at some point."

Because our relationship isn't as strong as it could be, I don't feel I can tell him that it's time for him to grow up. I don't think he'll be receptive because we're more of good acquaintances than friends. Of course, now that I'm thinking about it, I might look for an opportunity to share my concerns with him soon...because I know it is what is best for him, and I would want someone to do that for me.

Summary

If you're that immature guy, quit being that guy. You're not a bum. Man up. Or woman up. The time for many of the young people in our country to grow up is *now*.

Respect yourself enough to start doing the things you know you need to do. Do not put off until tomorrow what you can start doing today.

If you are mature but have close friends that are still living years behind where they need to be, start looking for ways to lovingly (or sometimes bluntly) challenge them to grow. Don't beat them over the head or preach at them nonstop. Like my friend did for me, just show them the light, and let them choose.

You have choices to make, decisions to be made.

You have a future, and *you* have the greatest impact on what your life will become. I'm in your corner, and I'm rooting for you.

"You never really understand a person until you consider things from his point of view... Until you climb inside of his skin and walk around in it."

— Harper Lee, *To Kill a Mockingbird*

"You don't know what you into down here...when you're guilty from the moment you're born."

— Jamie Foxx in *Just Mercy*

Chapter 7
Racism Isn't Much of an Issue Anymore.

It is true that racism is not as prevalent as it used to be. The bold, angry protests by whites against darker skinned people that were regular across the South a few short decades ago have virtually dried up. School integration, equal voting rights and other common civil rights have been decided and accepted by the overwhelming majority of Americans. Also, mixed-race couples are not only ordinary in cities, but growingly more commonplace across rural America.

All of this is great news, of course. This is such significant progress that many white folks are eager to move on like racism is no longer an issue. After all, details of America's racist history are not only shameful and embarrassing, they can be very unsettling and even horrific to discuss and ponder.

In fact, much of the racial tension today is perpetuated by affirmative action challenges and minorities crying, "Racist!" at minor things when most of the time, there wasn't even a racial motive. Right?

Stop.

Think about it.

In reading that italicized paragraph, what did you feel?

45

What do you think about those words… "affirmative action," and, "minorities crying, 'Racist!'"?

It's likely that you have strong feelings. Either you have strong feelings of anger toward me for writing that. Or you have a strong feeling of agreement like, "Yes, exactly!"

I am white. For much of my life, I fell into the latter category, the, "Yes, exactly!"

Now, older, wiser and having much more life experience, I definitely can't read the italicized paragraph without feeling anger starting to well up in me.

My feelings have markedly shifted. This was due to a number of life experiences, but perhaps none greater than when my own children faced racism and the helplessness I felt as their father and protector.

My perceptions of race relations and tensions, like yours, began before I was aware, even before I was born. Yes, the seeds of how you view different races and race issues were planted and growing *before* you were even born. (I'm not saying that just because your grandfather was racist, you are destined to be racist too, but I am suggesting that the people you grow up around have one of the greatest influences on your life.)

My own father is Italian. His late parents are Italian. At least two of my father's Italian grandparents were born in Sicily and immigrated to the United States through Ellis Island. Later my grandparents moved to Tampa, Florida. My dad was born in Tampa, and so was I.

I'm not exactly sure when or where the prejudice toward black people on that side of the family began, but I know that in New York in

46

decades past, Italians and the black community didn't get along. This racial depiction in the movie *A Bronx Tale* is portrayed more accurately than one might expect.[3]

Adding fuel to the already heated prejudicial fire, my great uncle was robbed at gunpoint at his store by a black man. I'm sure I heard him and my grandfather use the N-word once or twice. I remember my mother having a heated conversation with my grandfather once about this and not using that word around his grandchildren.

I heard different comments from different family members and friends about people based on race (and politics and religion and class, etc., but the focus in this chapter is race). Some comments were negative. Some were positive. I remember the first racial joke I heard. I remember the embarrassed face of the Indian girl who was listening. We were in fourth grade. Then, there was the TV, movies and news feeding me a number of additional racial messages as I grew up in the 80s and 90s.

I had no consciousness of it then, but my perception of race relations-or my prejudices-was being formed for me.

I remember kids at a school in Tampa talking about how white kids had to earn a higher GPA to be on honor roll but minority kids could be on honor roll with a lower GPA. I recall my dad being frustrated at the bidding process for jobs because his company had to go out of its way to find minority owned businesses to bid. And after my first year of college, I remember my church friend telling me how she attended the University of Florida and received a check for a large sum of money each semester from all her scholarships. She was smart. She was a girl. She was African, not African-American, but like from

Kenya, African. I was so frustrated to hear that. I was smart, but I was a white male and had to take out student loans, even after scholarships I had received, to the tune of tens of thousands of dollars.

All of this was just not fair. And so, my victim mentality was fed.

I played basketball all the time throughout my youth. It wasn't unusual for me to be the only "white dude" on the court. The N-word was used all the time, but 99% of the time I heard it, it was on the basketball court and not in a way that offended anyone. It was primarily used by guys of color. Growing up, I heard that word in the context of a white person intending to demean a black person very few times.

I had a few black friends. We'd hang out here and there. I balled with black kids all the time. With the exception of a couple comments by my granddad when I was young and one or two white trash types I came across growing up, I didn't see racism. As far as I was aware, racism didn't really exist any longer.

Oh, to be young and naive...

In the fall of 1999, I began college in a small town in Tennessee, and that's when I started to get my first real hints that racism was still alive. I remember asking a white friend of mine who lived in Georgia to invite a mutual friend (of color) home on one of our school breaks. He was reluctant, and when I finally pushed him on it, he said that his family is from the deep south and he didn't think they'd appreciate it. I had a hard time wrapping my brain around that.

Another friend from Florida had declined to come up to Tennessee when our high school friend group came to visit. Later, I realized she didn't feel safe traveling to Tennessee as a person of color.

After seeing black people in the college yearbook, she did come visit on another trip.

After 9/11, the tension around any middle eastern looking man in the area was palpable. One of my friends who is Israeli, while fishing at a church pond where the pastor allowed him to fish, was asked if he was a terrorist multiple times by a redneck neighbor partly because my friend "had a beard," which obviously means he wanted to fly an airplane into our small town courthouse (insert eye roll emoji here).

One of the most chilling conversations I've ever had was with my neighbor Cecil after I graduated from college. He was an old hunched over fellow who moved slowly. His skin had been weathered by, I suppose, too many years in the sun. I'm not sure how, but our conversation turned towards the topic of race. Then he asked me a question that I'll never forget.

"Have you ever been to a hang'n?"

It seemed like time stopped for a bit. The thought of a real live "hang'n" was something that I don't think I ever truly let my mind dwell on much. I had seen pictures, and I remember how gut-wrenching the movie *Amistad* was, but a real person...You mean, a real human being was actually chased down, thrown to the ground, had his, or her, hands tied behind his back, a noose put around his neck, and...

I think that was the first time I ever intentionally thought of a human being, with flesh and blood, with hair and teeth, with a family, tangibly warm to the touch and later cold to the touch–being murdered by other human beings in such a terrifying fashion. And from historic photos, many children firsthand witnessed this type of brutality. Many people cheered the savage events.

"No...no," I said horrified. "No."

"I have," Cecil responded.

There was pain and shame in his voice. It was almost like a confession. I didn't ask for details. I don't know what part he did or did not play. I don't know if he was four, fourteen, or forty-four years old when this happened. What I do know is that he carried it with him for the rest of his life.

And then it hit me...

He wasn't the victim. The victim likely wasn't even someone he cared about. Not his friend. Not his family. Not his race. And this had scarred him for decades.

What about the victim?

What about him? Or her?

What about the family?

What about his race? How many people alive today have had a traumatic experience in which someone's life was threatened or heinously taken simply because of the color of their skin?

How do you protect your family? What do you tell them if this is a possibility?

Do Americans remember the lynching of 17-year old Jesse Washington in 1917? Or the brutal murder of 14-year old Emmett Till in 1955? Or how the governor of Mississippi shook the hand of Medgar Evers's assassin at trial in the 1960s before an acquittal? Or how white supremacists dragged James Byrd to death in 1998? Or how Ahmaud Arbery was shot and killed while out for a jog in 2020?

Do white Americans remember?

I don't think I'm going out on a limb to suggest that minorities likely recall these among countless other tragedies much more than

50

white Americans. And I think the reason is simple. It hits much closer to home for some, more than others.

I've been pulled over by the cops probably a dozen times or so, but I've never been scared that I might be mistreated based on my race. I've been to the store thousands of times, and I hardly ever wondered if the cashier or a manager or another customer might treat me condescendingly based on the color of my skin. I take these things for granted.

It never really occurred to me.

Then, my former spouse, my three children and I moved to Botswana to serve on a mission there for 15 months.

Botswana is in southern Africa, just above South Africa. It is a beautiful country with beautiful people. Many things were wonderful. However, my son stopped wanting to go to school. He began crying every night, begging not to go back to school. Days turned to weeks. Weeks eventually turned to months. Holding your crying son every night because he now hates going to school is a painful and impactful experience.

The long story short is he was the only white kid in his class. His teacher was not a fan of white people, and in her defense, she probably had good reason. She was mistreating him. Eventually, changes were made, and there was a resolution.

I've grieved this for my son over the years. I think the effects probably linger today, many years later. Why couldn't I protect him better? I'm his father. My job is to protect and provide. I failed to protect him. I failed to provide a safe environment.

This kinda haunts me, even to this day.

And as I dwell on this, it occurs to me that while my family suffered a painful race-related experience, it pales in comparison to the horrors that thousands, rather millions, of minority men, women and children have faced over the recent decades...or rather, over the centuries.

The wounds of my situation haven't yet completely healed. How much longer will the scars of significantly greater tragedies that occurred over generations take to heal? How long will it take for that fear to be replaced by peace? More importantly, how long will it take for prejudicial thoughts, attitudes and behavior to be replaced by kindness and acceptance of those who look differently?

How many times have you heard someone start a conversation or a joke with, "I'm not racist, but..."?

Do me a favor. Next time you hear that opening, cut them off right there. Ninety-nine percent of people using that disclaimer are about to say something that will perpetrate racist thinking. That laugh is NOT worth the damage.

Just say, "No thanks, I don't want to hear it," and walk away like a superhero, because, in that moment, you are.

Summary

While there has been notable progress in the area of race, racism is still a major issue in the United States. Racial perceptions are influenced greatly by the generations before us, comments they made, what shows they let us watch, who they raised us around and their own biases. A few hundred years of an entrenched racist mindset, actions and government policies will not simply disappear after a handful of years of affirmative action and some people standing up for equality. While we want to move on, we must not forget the past; neither should we live in it. Acknowledge the past. Get to know people who are different. Be kind. Give others the benefit of the doubt. If or when you have children, teach them to have respect for others who are different, look different and sound different. Live peacefully. Smile. Go out of your way to do random acts of kindness for others of another race. Don't be kind out of guilt or a condescending attitude or because you feel sorrow for someone. Do it because our country, our world, has a major wound that is still healing, and you can help the process.

Homework assignment: Tonight or tomorrow, pick one of these movies (I recommend *Best of Enemies*) based on a true story and watch it with a friend or your family (or by yourself if no one's available). Good movies have a way of bringing events to life that make it easier to understand and appreciate. You will be a better person for it.

Title	Year	Rating	Comments
Ghosts of Mississippi[4]	1996	PG-13	This is the story of trying to get justice for the murder of Medgar Evers over 20 years after the crime was committed.
42[5]	2013	PG-13	The story of Jackie Robinson is a movie every American should know and every baseball and civil rights fan should watch. (Much of it was filmed near where I live and some people I know are extras in the film.)

Selma[6]	2014	PG-13	At the height of the civil rights movement, MLK joins the fight for equal voting rights for Blacks in Alabama and across the South.
Hidden Figures[7]	2016	PG	This film recounts the lives of black women whose math skills helped NASA put the first man in space.
The Green Book[8]	2018	PG-13	An Italian tough guy escorts a black musician as his bodyguard on a tour through the South in the 1960s.
Just Mercy[2]	2019	PG-13	Walter McMillian was arrested and put on death row for murder. Attorney Bryan Stevenson fights to have the conviction overturned.
Best of Enemies[9]	2018	PG-13	Do yourself a favor. Do NOT watch the trailer. This story is so incredible that no one would believe it if it were not true. School integration, the KKK and a feisty civil rights leader converge in 1971 Durham, NC.
Till[10]	2022	PG-13	The lynching of 14-year old Emmett Till was a brutal, horrific murder. I'll let you decide for yourself if you watch this movie, but Americans at least need to know this story.

"Give a man a fish, feed him for a day. Teach a man to fish, feed him for life."

– Unknown

Chapter 8
The government will take care of you.

Disclaimer: this is not a political chapter; there is no other agenda here outside of speaking the truth.

"Okay, so here's what you can do," the voice on the other line said confidently. "Enroll at college. Take another class, even if it's just one. Then apply for financial aid. Consolidate your old student loans and your new loans. Make the minimum payment for 10 years, and then you can apply for forgiveness!"

The woman to whom I was speaking worked for a company involved in student loan forgiveness. This was her bright idea, and there was even excitement in her voice, like she had made some kind of genius discovery. I had been in contact with her through a friend whom I trust. This was sometime around 2014, and I had been repaying my student loans for *10 years already.*

Working in education, I heard of student loan forgiveness programs for...teachers. My former spouse and I had consolidated some of our student loans, and we had roughly another 20 years to pay on them at the time. Of the approximately $60,000 in loans we had, $5,000 had already been forgiven. I definitely appreciated that. However, after 10 years of paying over $300 a month, I was hopeful the rumors I'd been hearing about total teacher loan forgiveness were true.

But they were not. At least not for me. Every person's loan situation is unique, and I did not meet the criteria. Many don't. So the advice I received was to borrow more money, dig myself a larger financial hole, lower my monthly payments, pay the minimum payment for an additional 10 years (or at least 120 payments of hundreds of dollars), so that I can then apply for forgiveness, of which she was *"pretty sure"* (but not certain) I'd receive.

Ho-ly cow! This lady was actually serious!

Now, you might be thinking that her plan *could* have been a decent option.

Let me just share a few thoughts to address that idea.

One, I applied for, signed and promised to pay my loans back. They were my responsibility. If there were a program to help, great, but I wasn't going to try to *game* the system like that.

Two, this might have been fraud. Even if it didn't meet the legal criteria for fraud, morally, it just seems wrong.

Three, who wants debt hanging around their neck for over another decade? Another option would have been to double my payments and have paid it off in five years to regain my freedom; however, I don't think this option was even on her radar. Her mindset was all about trying to extract from the government, even if doing so would prolong one's financial and mental stress.

And four, who do I want in control of my destiny: the government or me? I chose me then. I choose me now. And just in case you have any doubt, I choose me in the future. I'm not perfect, but neither is our government. While I maintain a healthy respect for the United States government, it is far from perfect. There could be three different presidents, hundreds of different congressmen, thousands of bills passed and dozens of policy changes in the course of a decade. As a general rule that I follow (and I suggest you do also if you have the ability), when deciding between potential government relief years down the road or cleaning up my own mess now, I choose me.

I can think of very few more helpless phases of life than depending on the government to take care of you. If you have reached the point where you are dependent on the government, one of two things has likely happened: either your plans have been utterly derailed or you had a really, really bad plan from the start. There is another option of mental or physical disability, but that makes up an extreme minority of cases.

Most people don't plan to attain complete dependency on the government, but there are many people who actively take advantage of government programs, loopholes, laws and policies as part of their overall future outlook.

For example, when I adopted one of my kids, I heard about a generous tax refund. By the time the adoption was completed the laws had changed and the refund was significantly less, in our case about 80% less. When I asked why, the person at the agency explained that people had been legally (but not really) adopting grandchildren, nieces and nephews, etc. and sharing the refund among family members. Wow!

Many people lie on their taxes. I just had a conversation with a man who referees. He told me he was frustrated because he had worked at one school so much that the principal gave him a 1099 last year, so now he had to claim all that income. When I was a server in college, the manager advised me "off the record" that I could claim 10% of my tips as opposed to my actual tips. Some people lie about their income to get a higher pell grant for college, food stamps or government housing. Other people intentionally try to stay at low-to-no income to legitimately receive government assistance. And some wealthier people try to hide or move income and assets illegally to keep from paying the full taxes on it.

The concept of leveraging, or defrauding in some instances, what the government has to offer is not new; however, the frequency and degree to which people are actively trying to take advantage of the government is growing rapidly. And what's really alarming, and dangerous, is that some people's habits and lifestyle of taking advantage of the government is leading to their dependency on the government.

Let me be clear. There is a definite difference between people who legally and legitimately make the most of programs when available and people who are trying to exploit and dishonestly take advantage of the government to provide the majority of their needs.

Now, I am all for the government helping people who *need* help. There are many people who genuinely need assistance like those with physical or mental disabilities, orphaned children, people who are at or below the poverty line, and others. However, the goal of government assistance should be to move people towards independence, not keeping them dependent by rewarding behaviors that are counterproductive.

Simply put–when people receive a reward, they have a tendency to repeat what they did. This is true for both positive and negative behaviors. This is why many good teachers use candy, clips or other positive reinforcement to get most students to behave well in class.

You can see the opposite of this with some parenting styles. For instance, have you ever noticed the kid who begs for their parents attention only to be constantly ignored until the child has an outburst? Then, the parent starts reprimanding the child. The child cries. The parent puts their arm around the child and says the child is tired, not feeling well or makes some other excuse. If the parent never addresses the child's need for attention and how to communicate this appropriately, these temper tantrums for attention can become frequent. If this cycle continues, the child becomes an overdramatic kid who regularly throws fits. This is learned behavior, even though the child is unaware of what is happening.

Here are some examples of how poor government programs, regulations and laws reinforce people being dependent on the government. Single parents (most of whom are single moms) often have a significantly greater tax advantage if they stay single. Food stamps in some states can last indefinitely if one meets the income guidelines. Parents who foster will often lose government assistance if the family legally adopts the child. Unemployment will often be paid for six months to a year...if the person stays unemployed. The government has also protected private student loan providers allowing them to offer absurd loan amounts that cannot be bankrupted. Finally, many people save and invest very little, thinking that they'll live on social security after they retire only to realize later how great the difference is between what they will actually receive and how much they will need.

Let me ask you a question, "What is the purpose of our government?"

How would you answer that?

Would you say, "to take care of its people"?

Some people might.

I would argue that from a historical (not political) perspective, the purpose of the United States government is to give people the *freedom* to take care of themselves.

The Preamble to the United States Constitution lays out five specific purposes: *"establish Justice, insure domestic Tranquility, provide for the common defense, promote the general Welfare, and secure the Blessings of Liberty to ourselves and our Posterity."*[1]

Those are some large vocabulary words even for a teacher, so here's my attempt at a simple paraphrase:

1. We have laws to provide justice and fairness.
2. We have laws to provide for peaceful living within our country.
3. We have a military to protect us from outside attack.
4. The government should promote what's in the public interest and common good.
5. The government ensures our freedom will be protected for future generations.

I don't see anything there that says the government should support everybody. In fact, I interpret this as saying that the purpose of our government is to provide a country in which you can take care of yourself and I can take care of myself.

And that's not a bad thing. In fact, I personally take it as a compliment. My government is not going to enable me nor disempower me. My government provides a free high school diploma (and in 35 states free community college) and allows me the freedom to make my own decisions and provide for myself and my family.[2] While schooling is a major help, it's not the government's responsibility to raise my

60

children and teach them to become productive members of society. It's my responsibility. I like it that way. I *prefer* it that way.

I encourage you to be the person in control of your destiny. Don't expect the government to take care of you.

Summary

It is not the United States government's responsibility to take care of you. There are benefits and programs that exist to help those in need and even some that help those who are not really in need. That's wonderful. Take advantage of what you legally can; however, don't become dependent on the government. Don't seek to manipulate the government into giving you handouts and staying dependent. In fact, do the opposite: strive to become independent. Get your free high school diploma, but more importantly, learn while you're there. Get an education, certificate or degree to work doing something you enjoy. Save some money. Put some in a retirement plan *every* paycheck. If the economy dips or the government malfunctions, *you* won't need to worry because *you* took the steps to provide stability for *your* future. You have that freedom. You have that privilege. You will respect yourself more and sleep better knowing that *you* are in control of your destiny and you don't have to rely on politicians.

"And he started walking forward when coach finished. And you can tell that he was respected because there was an obvious reverence for this African American pastor. And when he got close to coach, coach could see him. He had tears on his face, and he said, 'I never thought in my lifetime that I would hear a white man say the things that you said."

— Dr. Raleigh Washington
(referring to how people were impacted when Colorado Buffalo head coach Bill McCartney traveled the country addressing racial reconciliation and apologizing to black men for how they'd been treated by white men)[1]

Chapter 9
Racism in America hasn't improved.

At first glance this chapter might seem to contradict a previous chapter; however, once both are read fully, doubts of conflict will be replaced with understanding.

Yes, racism is still an issue in America. Don't believe the lie that the issue is entirely behind us. However, be careful also not to believe the lie that there has not been significant progress.

Racism is a highly sensitive, delicate and complex issue. It punishes certain people and benefits others. Some people feel it all the time yet others don't even notice it. Some celebrate racial diversity while others are gripped by fear in racially diverse situations.

Prejudice takes many forms and impacts certain people groups. Women, blacks, the elderly, Hispanics, the physically challenged and physically deformed, Jews, the poor, the homeless, Asians, those who are short and a host of other people groups have all felt the brunt of prejudice, but none perhaps as much in recent history as minorities.

Racism is a dark, uncomfortable, undeniable, ugly and despicable part of American history. If we don't talk about it enough, we are in danger of forgetting. If we study it in too much detail, we find ourselves possibly getting sick to our stomachs, growing resentment, burning with anger, questioning God, harboring strong negative feelings for too long or a combination of these.

However, the good news is that the issue of racism in our country has improved greatly and continues to improve. I had not noticed this until I lived outside the United States for an extended period. Ironically, I learned this in the heart of Africa.

In 2015, my family and I moved to Maun, Botswana, to work with Love Botswana Outreach Mission. We served for 15 months, and I loved it. I had different goals, but along the way, I learned quite a bit about prejudice–much more than our limited American perspective allows us.

First of all, I was a minority. I am white, and the town, and country at large, is full of people with very dark skin and features. In fact, at one village we visited we got off a bus, and a lady we were with burst out laughing.

When I asked why, she translated that the children were yelling to each other, "Let's go see the white people! Let's go see the white people!" in Setswana as they all came running.

More often than not, my being a minority in Botswana was a benefit. There were a handful of times, however, that my being white brought negative experiences. Getting pulled over by the police was a guaranteed ticket. (I was speeding, and that's on me.) Trying to barter in the market was a challenge as I felt I was always charged quite a bit more than the locals for various items. I received a number of unkind looks from a number of men who likely had previous negative experiences with people of my skin color. All of these, however, were fairly minor compared to my son being harassed by his teacher.

Aside from the issue with the teacher, these were relatively minor and didn't significantly affect my life. However, I also have a daughter who I adopted from China. She's the same to me as my other kids, but she does look different. We had been challenged here and there with disparaging remarks made about Asians or Chinese people in the States. There is a similar attitude in Botswana but with another layer on top, because there is a section in town referred to as "the China shops" because Chinese people import and sell inexpensive things "Made in China." It wasn't all the time, but there were definitely running jokes and disparaging remarks about Chinese people.

I sat in a class taught by Gary Pelotshweu. PG, as he was affectionately called, is an engaging, humorous but tell-it-straight type of speaker. I listened with my complete attention as he talked to the form fives (seniors) about overcoming things that might hold them back. One point was about white people who would discriminate against them. No surprise here, but the next point is what shocked me: other black people that would discriminate against them.

I struggled with this. It took me quite some time to wrap my head around.

While in Botswana, I found PG and a number of other locals to be wise and valuable resources on a variety of topics, but especially on racism and discrimination.

For starters, I want to acknowledge that it is impossible to move across the globe, live somewhere for a year and be an expert on the dynamics and nuances of the community. I admit that my understanding is limited, but having had the opportunities to live in other countries (Argentina for a month, Ghana for almost three months and Botswana for 15 months), I feel my understanding is also greater than when I had only lived in the U.S.

One of the biggest issues on the planet of which I had no knowledge was tribalism. (I would prefer to use a different word than "tribalism," but this was the word used by the people in Maun to explain it to me, so I'll use it.) Tribalism is discrimination based on one's tribe.

I was informed that there are at least 8 distinct tribes in Botswana, and there is a very real but unwritten hierarchy: all native Batswana know which tribe is higher or lower than the next. The government has outlawed discrimination, but much like laws about discrimination in the U.S. have taken many decades to bring tangible and real change, so it is in other countries. (Prejudice isn't only an American issue; it's global.) Gaining independence in 1966, Botswana is relatively young, and while the Batswana are making progress, they still have a long way to go.

The more I learned about tribalism in Botswana, the more I began to research and discuss it with others from abroad. With over 3,000 different languages and tribes, tribalism is real and alive across Africa, but it is not limited to Africa. Tribalism extends throughout Central and South America, all throughout Asia and in Australia. A number of sources say tribalism as prejudice still even exists among Native (North) Americans and even in Europe.

Racism and tribalism are not the exact same thing, but they are similar. Both discriminate: one based on the culture you were born into and the other based on the physical characteristics you were born with.

Throughout my time abroad and personal research, I have learned a sad truth: in one form or another, discrimination has existed throughout most of human history across the globe.

This has made me reflect quite a bit on the issue of discrimination, particularly racism, in my country and in the city where I live.

Is racism gone? Definitely not!

Will it ever be completely eradicated? I hope so, but I doubt it.

Over the past decade or so, the media has actively reported on a string of stories about racism. The media's favorites seem to be if the police are involved. They get extra clicks the more shocking the title! While many of these stories are undeniably racist, there are some that if you read or review the facts with no knowledge of the skin color of anyone involved, the police acted appropriately (i.e. they would have done the same thing to a guy of their same skin color under the same circumstances).

I realize I might take heat for that last sentence, but I started this book by saying I cared enough about you to tell you the truth-even if you don't want to hear it.

The truth is that racism is still an issue in our country. All of us need to recognize that and be sensitive to it.

As a white person, I need to be and should be conscious that others have been heavily wounded by people with my color of skin because of their color of skin. I can be active in making sure I don't condone racist jokes or comments and intentionally broadening my circle of people to include people of color.

People of color can be more intentional about not using the race card anytime something bad happens. People of color can provide a little more grace for silly white people who act scared or startled when a person of color walks by. Instead of sneering at them, maybe just smirk or give a small laugh at their ignorance.

The truth is also that racism in America is improving. There are many more mixed couples today than there were when I was growing up. Racist crimes have decreased. The percentage of minorities in America with a college degree has grown significantly in recent decades. Finally, the United States of America has now had both a president and a vice president of color.

Summary

Two things can be true. Racism is still an issue; but there have been significant improvements. Discrimination in all forms is unacceptable, and racism can be particularly horrific. It needs to be addressed. But don't think that discrimination is unique to America. In fact, you will find racism, tribalism and discrimination based on one's culture throughout history across the globe and alive in virtually every country. The media regularly tells us how awful racism in the U.S. is, but the reality is that many other countries are behind the U.S. as far as racial progress is concerned. America is on the right track. There is definitely still work to be done, but the truth is that America has indeed made significant progress. Let's continue the work of racial equality together with a more positive, hopeful outlook.

"I used to wonder why people seem like they are prisoners of their phones, but then it occurred to me that's why they're called 'cell' phones."

— dad joke

Chapter 10
You Need to Keep Your Phone on You
(for Emergencies).

I remember the first time I heard it. It was my junior year in the late 90's, and our friend group had been close for a number of years.

We attended a small school in Oldsmar, FL, and life was good. I played soccer in the fall and basketball in the winter, if you can call the handful of chilly days in Tampa that. I wore shorts on most Christmases.

Many of us had turned sixteen and finally had a set of wheels. A rich sophomore had a BMW. One of my best friends drove a Ford Expedition. One of the seniors rolled an Isuzu Trooper he cockily referred to as "the beach cruiser."

I drove my dad's old clunker around for a few months before I was able to buy my first car, a white Dodge Shadow. It didn't stay white for long. As soon as I had saved up $300 bucks or so, I had it painted bright lemon yellow. Later, I saved a couple more hundred dollars and put two 10" subwoofers in the back, which made the neighbors super happy!

Then, there was a girl who drove her dad's Oldsmobile. Thirty years ago, it was technically an antique, so that sucker would be like 50 years old today. It was massive! We were all sitting around one day, and boom, she dropped the mic (before such a phrase existed).

"My parents bought me a cell phone," she shared sheepishly, "But it's only for emergencies."

I had no idea how many times I'd hear "cell phone" and "for emergencies" used in the same sentence throughout the rest of my life. If you would have tried to warn me, I wouldn't have believed you anyway.

I teach sixth grade and roughly half of my students now have a personal cell phone, for "emergencies," of course.

I didn't own a cell phone until my junior year of college in 2002. And not only did that phone not connect to the internet or have apps, it didn't have a camera either. My parents didn't own a cell phone until they were in their forties, and my grandparents never owned a cell phone. Yet, we all lived.

Yes, I know the world has changed. Yes, I know it would be almost impossible to have any semblance of a normal life in modern society without a cell phone today. No, I am not suggesting that we revert to a time without cell phones, but what I am suggesting is that the use of cell phones has become so pervasive that, many times, the use of a cell phone is more detrimental than beneficial. In fact, many people are becoming addicted to cell phones so much that it is directly damaging the most important relationships in one's life.

The key is balance. There are times you need to have your phone on you. There are also times when you should put it away. There are even times when it would be best to turn it off for an hour, for a day or even a week.

Could you do that?

How does turning off your phone for an entire week sound to you?

A year or so ago, I went on a retreat in which it was required that I power my phone off for the entire three day period. I had to make a plan for my children. I took a personal day off work. I gave my wife a phone number to a leader that she could contact "in case of an emergency." Spoiler alert: she never used the number.

I must have reached in my pocket 100 times that weekend, and my hand came out empty-handed every single time. It was weird. It was a bit frustrating. It left me feeling a bit confused about the time, the weather, sports, social media and communication with friends and family. It was also sobering. It was also a way for me to prioritize. It was freeing. It was nice. It enabled me to focus 100% on my goals that weekend and to have zero distractions. It was refreshing, and it was empowering.

I survived.

Let me share a fascinating story from history with you that will shed some light on solutions and unintended consequences.

In colonial India, the British found the large number of venomous cobras in and around Delhi both unpleasant and dangerous. To decrease the population, the British government developed a program to pay people for dead cobras. At first, the initiative seemed to be a success; however, capitalists can be found all around the world. Savvy Indians began breeding the cobras to turn in dozens of snakes instead of just a couple. Of course, the program was canceled once word got out. With no more reward, the people let all their baby cobras go, and the result was a higher cobra population than there was at the beginning. Today, the term "cobra effect" is used when a solution makes the issue worse than the problem at the beginning.

This is clearly recognizable with social media. The irony of *social* media is that it has made humans much less social. What was created to connect people has backfired and left many people feeling more disconnected than they were, not to mention feeling more anxious and depressed.

According to Kevin Kamiyar, "Research has shown that people who spend more time on social media tend to have fewer close relationships and lower levels of social support than those who spend less time on these platforms."[1]

Experience confirms this research. How many times have you seen a couple on a date at a restaurant and both are looking at their phones instead of talking to each other? How many children are now neglected by their parents because their mom or dad spend more time on their phones than talking to them? Don't we all have that one family member that never gets off their phone, and she or he drives everyone nuts? (If you don't think your family does, maybe check the mirror? Just saying.)

It's not just social media. The problem is when people regularly prioritize their phone over those around them.

I attended a marriage conference where Jeremy Evans presented some thoughts and research on the issues with technology.[2] He shared many startling statistics about children and technology and spouses and technology. Some spouses actually check their phones during sex! Many spouses have either contemplated divorce or have filed for divorce over cell phone use and addiction. There is also a strong correlation between excessive time on technology and depression.

Evans said that, "Intimacy requires human contact."[2]

Isn't that true?

Children need physical touch. Google "Harry Harlow" if you would like some scientific research on it. Even teens and adults need physical touch.

Let me ask you a question.

Who do you touch more often than your phone?

Many people have gotten to the point where they touch their phone more than anything else or anyone else in the world. More than their spouse, their girlfriend or boyfriend, their parents or worse, their children.

While it is true that there are emergencies in the world, it is also true that you do NOT need your phone on you all the time. In fact, it will make your life better if you are intentional about having some phone-free time and space.

As a general rule at my house, my wife and I do not allow phones at the kitchen table. Sure, there are some exceptions, but in general, the table is a phone free zone. In my car on the way to and from school, the kids must put their phones away. This way I can ask them about their day. They can either talk to me or sit in silence. I used to have my phone plugged in where I could reach it in bed. I realized this had a negative effect on my marriage, so I moved it to the other side of the room. Yes, when my alarm goes off, I have to get up and walk a few steps to my phone...and my marriage is stronger for it. My children have parental controls on their phone. Also, I turned my email notifications off. I will check my email when I get to it a couple times a day (or not that day at all). Sure, I miss some things, but I am not missing out on as much engaged time with my family as I did.

Boundaries in life are healthy, and one of the most important areas is when it comes to your phone. Consider putting your phone away after school or work for an hour. Maybe your table should be a phone free zone? What if you left your phone in the car on dates? How much screen time do you use on an average day? How much is a healthy amount?

You need to create some healthy boundaries for your phone usage *today*. Talk with people you respect and trust. If you're married, discuss it with your spouse. Stop connecting with virtual reality so much and connect with real people again. Don't just be in the room. Make sure your mind is present. Raise your children with healthy screen habits.

Summary

Quit using the excuse that you need to have your phone on you all the time in case of emergencies. That's bologna! Yes, have your phone on you when you're on a long trip, at work if you need it, for directions and when you're going somewhere that might be unsafe. But also start creating phone free time and places. Do you control it, or does it control you? Like Neo in *The Matrix*, unplug yourself. Your phone is not more important than people. It's okay to go a couple hours or days or weeks without checking Tik-Tok or your favorite app. It's actually okay to go a few days without your phone at all. Be intentional about how you use, and don't use, your phone. Find balance and create some healthy boundaries.

Chapter 11
There are some things you don't have to forgive.

If you want to live life to the fullest, a life of freedom, then you cannot buy into the lie that it's okay *not* to forgive certain people or things.

I am aware that some people have experienced horrific violations, and if you're one of those, I might be about to lose you at that first sentence, but please...please stay with me and read this chapter through to the end. What do you have to lose? In fact, I would challenge you that if you already have feelings of anger stirring in you, then this might be the most important chapter you ever read. Don't skip it.

I want to share two stories with you from great men I admire from opposite sides of the globe. One was the victim of a terrible crime, and the other was the victim of extreme injustice for 70 years.

Growing up, I was a huge Florida State University (FSU) Seminoles football fan and a die-hard Tampa Bay Buccaneers fan. Rooting for a player who was dominant on both teams was extremely rare, so when I watched Warrick Dunn juking defenders on Saturdays and then on Sundays, he quickly became one of my favorite athletes.

In high school I heard "feel good" stories on the news about Dunn buying houses for single moms and thought, "That's nice," and never thought much more of it until one time I heard why.

On January 5, 1993, Warrick Dunn celebrated his 18th birthday. Two days later, the phone rang in the middle of the night. His mom Betty Smothers, a police officer, had been shot while working a second job as a security guard. Being the oldest of the six children, Dunn was picked up by an officer and rushed to the hospital. Betty was pronounced dead, and as the only family member at the hospital at the time, Dunn was asked to verify her body, with bandages around her head from the gunshot wound.

Not only was Warrick Dunn orphaned by murder, but so were his five younger siblings. Betty never saw Warrick or any of his five siblings graduate. She never saw any of her kids go to college, get married or have children.

As for Warrick, she never watched him beat the Florida Gators or Miami Hurricanes as a Seminole. She wasn't there when he won NFL Offensive Rookie of the Year, was voted to the Pro Bowl, won the Walter Man of the Year Award or for any of his other accomplishments. Warrick fell into depression.

On the outside, Warrick appeared to have it all: success, millions of dollars, good looks, a cut physique, and he was a superstar athlete! But as he reveals in his book *Running for My Life*, Dunn was caught blindside by his teammate who asked him why he never looked happy or could look anyone in the eye.[1] It had been years since his mother's murder, and despite the money, fame and success, Warrick still had not recovered from the violence two thieves had inflicted on his family that dreadful night over a decade before.

The second story which unfolded in Africa is, in some ways, even more heart wrenching. After years of colonization, slavery and war over land, gold and diamonds, the young nation of South Africa was born. Shortly thereafter, the racial Apartheid laws were passed discriminating against "blacks" and favoring "whites."

As the discrimination and crimes lasted for decades against his race, Nelson Mandela joined resistance groups. He was arrested and jailed multiple times for various reasons. Some reasons were legit; others were suspect. Eventually, Mandela was sentenced to life in jail for sabotage. (The United Nations, and many individual nations, publicly condemned the trial.) At the time, Mandela had a wife and five children.

Mandela spent 18 years at the infamous Robben Island prison where he was allowed one 30-minute visitor annually and allowed to write and receive one letter every six months. In case that did not sink in, reread it. *A human being was allowed one visitor once a year for only 30 minutes–for 18 years.* Mandela's cell was nine feet long and seven feet wide. That is 63 square feet. Most restrooms are larger than that. Eighteen years. Sixty-three square feet of living space.

Finally Mandela got off Robben Island…to spend an additional nine years in other prisons. His children were 27 years older by the time he was released from prison. His marriage, having suffered nearly three decades of prison, ended in divorce.

If anyone has a right to be bitter, angry and resentful, Warrick Dunn and Nelson Mandela are more than qualified, but both chose another way.

I remember the first time I read Dunn's story. I sat in a waiting room for a doctor appointment, and I picked up a magazine. (This was before phones had the internet or apps.) I started reading an article about one of my sports heroes, but it wasn't a sports story. It was the story of Dunn going to Angola prison in Louisiana to face one of his mom's killers on death row. It captivated me.

Then I read those words. Words no one in the room expected to hear. Words that sent tears down every man's face in that jailroom.

"I forgive you."

I've since read Dunn's book and watched him interviewed multiple times. Those words are still just as powerful. This man murdered Dunn's mom. This man stole her from her children for the rest of their lives. This man sentenced those six children to years, or lifetimes, of trauma.

Warrick Dunn forgave this man.

One of the great ironies is that Dunn's forgiveness was a turning point in which Dunn also received his own freedom. Dunn had more peace, felt like a weight lifted and smiled more.

Likewise, Nelson Mandela chose forgiveness over resentment, bitterness and hate and also found freedom, reminding us all that, "Forgiveness liberates the soul."

Mandela's accomplishments are too numerous to list, but some of the most notable are becoming the first black president of South Africa, president of the African National Congress and Nobel Peace Prize winner.

As a direct result of Mandela's forgiveness and attitude toward healing and unity, the nation of South Africa grew to be a leader in humanitarian progress throughout the continent and world. Sure there have been–and will continue to be–bumps along the way, but South Africa's leadership and resulting productivity is outstanding considering the nation's recent history and compared to the surrounding nations. South Africa is a leading global producer in gold, fruit, vehicle manufacturing, platinum, wine, tourism, diamonds and other goods. As of this writing, South Africa is the only African nation to have hosted a FIFA World Cup.

"Had Mandela chosen not to forgive?" one might ask.

The answer is easy. It happened right next door. Robert Mugabe ruled Zimbabwe out of bitterness and resentment for decades, and the country has struggled since. Conversely, South Africa has blossomed. I've visited both countries. My experience in South Africa was typical of what one who travels would expect. I've also shopped in a Zimbabwean grocery with pockets stuffed full of cash because everything in the store cost hundreds of thousands of Zim due to inflation. The economic instability of Zimbabwe was so bad that the Zim has since been demonetized...but you can still find the notes on eBay if you're interested.

Let me share one final story of how unforgiveness can hold you back.

I heard this story at a marriage conference, and I'll paraphrase it the best I can from my notes and memory.

A young couple had attended premarital counseling, and everything seemed normal to the counselor. He was in shock at the story that was revealed in his office several weeks after their wedding. After minutes had gone by and neither spouse wanting to reveal the reason for this mysterious appointment, eventually one spouse blurted out, "We haven't had sex!"

The counselor, in obvious surprise and confusion, began asking questions and prodding to get to the root of the matter. The couple had been physical before they were married, but they had always stopped short of "going all the way." Eventually, it was revealed that the wife had been the victim of long term sexual abuse and molestation at the hands of her grandfather. When she got under the covers naked with her husband, she couldn't shake the memories. The trauma would come back with intense pain and grip her with fear.

The husband was obviously torn and at a loss, not wanting to victimize his wife but also frustrated that roughly a couple months into his marriage, the marriage vows still remained unconsummated. The counseling session lasted well past the allotted time when the counselor finally dropped the bomb.

"You have to forgive your grandpa," he said. "If you ever want a normal marriage with your husband, you'll have to forgive your grandfather."

These were not the words the wife wanted to hear, but she was also in a place with absolutely zero direction on how to move forward. A short time later the counselor saw the husband and asked how things were. With a glow and a smile, the husband responded that things were "much better" with appreciation in his voice.

His wife had chosen to do the ugly, hard, painful and seemingly unfair work of forgiving, healing and letting go so she could move on with her life to the fullest.[2]

Now, please do not misunderstand me. I am not saying that forgiveness is easy. I am not blaming you for someone's sins against you. In that case, you are the victim. You may have been treated unfairly, disgracefully, grossly, shamefully, abusively, violently and even worse. I don't know your story, but I've met many people, including some of my students, who have had awful, horrific things happen to them. And I will give you all the same advice. If you want your best life moving forward, then you will need to forgive those who hurt you.

Forgiveness is *not* telling them that it's okay. In fact it is not okay.

Forgiveness is *not* letting them off the hook. In many instances, people should be punished to the fullest extent of the law.

Forgiveness is *not* weakness. Forgiveness is strength.

Forgiveness is *not* total forgetfulness. In fact, some things shouldn't be forgotten so history doesn't repeat itself. On the other hand, there might be some things that would be best forgotten.

Forgiveness is *not* letting them back into your life if they should be kept out. It is possible to forgive someone and also have a boundary in which you don't communicate with that person anymore. Reestablishing a relationship is reconciliation, and that is different from forgiveness. In some instances, reconciliation is an acceptable path forward, and in some instances, reconciliation should not even be an option.

Forgiveness is not always going up to someone and saying that you forgive them (although there are times this may be a good idea). Some people might respond in laughter or annoyance. Forgiveness can take a number of forms. It often comes after an apology, but there are also many times when no apology will be offered.

Forgiveness is *not* holding yourself back. Forgiveness is a step in the healing process. It allows you to move forward. It gives you your freedom back.

Forgiveness is recognizing that something very bad occurred to you. It is acknowledging who hurt you. It is saying that you will no longer dwell on it, that you will no longer remain bitter and resentful, that you will not seek vengeance, that you will no longer give the crime against you any power, and that you are moving on. Forgiveness gives you the power back. It allows you to control your destiny. It frees you from the prison you were in.

There are also physical benefits to forgiveness. According to an article by John Hopkins, "Studies have found that the act of forgiveness can reap huge rewards for your health, lowering the risk of heart attack; improving cholesterol levels and sleep; and reducing pain, blood pressure, and levels of anxiety, depression and stress."[3]

Some people might be able to forgive more easily. For many, forgiveness takes a significant amount of time in counseling, prayer, soul searching, healing and/or recovery. Forgiveness isn't for everyone. It's only for those who desire to grow, find freedom and get on with their lives in the best possible way. I pray that forgiveness is in your future.

<u>Summary</u>

This chapter began with the quote, "Unforgiveness is like drinking poison and expecting the other person to die." There are many variations of this quotation, but they all mean the same thing: holding onto unforgiveness doesn't harm the other person. In fact, it harms you. I know it can be painful, immensely painful. However, I care enough about you to tell you that learning to forgive is in your best interest. Forgiving will help old wounds heal. It will make you a better person and put you back in control of your future. It's not easy, but you are stronger than you know. You *can* be the bigger person. You *can* forgive that person.

Chapter 12
Toxic, internal lies.

There is counseling in which a guy goes into an office, lays on the couch, shares his problems, gets up in an hour and comes back a couple weeks later to do it all again. Then there's the intense, pay thousands of dollars, travel hours to an isolated place with professionals, turn in your phone for the week and get-ready-to-share-your-life-story counseling.

It was at the latter type that I realized just how powerful and lasting messages shared with people at a young age can be.

Dave was a typical dude. He was good-looking, confident and fun to be around. He was married to an attractive woman. Things were great early on, but after a while the grind of life started taking its toll on the young couple. Communication was not their strong point, and life together became challenging. Other women would regularly smile at Dave, and he began to appreciate their attention more than he should.

Dave shared how one of the biggest problems was that sometimes his wife would call him a liar. He went on to explain that when he was lying, this didn't bother him. It was the times that she had accused him of lying and he had not lied that really cut and caused him to have this growing resentment of his wife. When questioned further, it was revealed that he didn't really try to explain the truth to his wife.

In his mind, she thought he was lying, so that was the end of it. He just shut his mouth, buried it inside and resented the heck out of his wife for it.

A good bit of time later, Dave also shared a story of when he was a boy. His mother asked Dave and his brother which kid did something wrong (a rather shameful thing). Dave denied it, but then his older brother jumped in and said that Dave was lying and that Dave did it. His mother took the older son's word, accused Dave of lying and refused to let him even discuss it. In his mom's mind, Dave lied. Dave got punished. Dave was not allowed to talk about it. Case closed.

As Dave shared this experience, everyone could see that Dave had been absolutely devastated by the situation and was still carrying the pain over 20 years later.

From the outside, many people can connect the dots from these two significant episodes in Dave's life, but Dave didn't notice. Dave is a smart guy, but he didn't have a clue that the incident from his childhood had a major detrimental impact on how he communicates, or fails to communicate, with his wife today.

Dave had a deep wound, which had never healed. From this wound grew an internal lie that he unknowingly began to believe. Dave believed the lie that he has no voice and the women closest to him won't listen. In his mind, when the woman Dave cares about the most accuses him of lying, the issue is over and resolved: he may not talk about it anymore. At this point, he became completely powerless.

Dave had been married for at least five years, and his wife had accused him multiple times of lying. Sometimes, he indeed had. Then he would apologize, and they would move on. However, there were a number of times that Dave hadn't lied, and there was a perfectly reasonable explanation for the miscommunication. Unfortunately, Dave never knew how to explain the truth to his wife in these circumstances. He felt that he didn't have a voice. He always just shut his mouth, withdrew emotionally from his wife and unknowingly fed the bitterness towards her.

I don't know for sure what happened with Dave and his wife, but I am confident that with this revelation, Dave and his wife at least had the opportunity to communicate better, be more understanding and begin to heal the hurt and bitterness in their marriage if they both wanted.

I personally have a similar scar that I realized when I was about 30. It has to do with being falsely accused, of anything, not just lying. Sometimes, I would just emotionally detach, and other times I felt so angry, that I'd blow up and yell back like my life was in danger. I am a textbook example of going into fight or flight mode. I believed the lie that when I was falsely accused, I was helpless and defenseless. I can vividly recall the childhood experience that caused me to start believing this lie. For the most part, I react more maturely and graciously in these situations nowadays, but I have to admit that, sometimes, I still default to believing that ugly old lie about myself. It's not pretty, but I'm a work in progress. I keep moving forward.

I have heard dozens of adults say things like, "I'm not a good speaker."

"I'm not good at math."

"I'm just a little ole' hillbilly; what do I know?"

What's really heartbreaking is when you hear someone say, "No one could ever love someone like me." Or, "I'm too damaged to ever get married." Or, "I don't want to have kids because I know I could never be a good parent."

I remember a conversation towards the end of my senior year of high school that left a big impression on me. I went to a very small high school, and many of the students had known each other for years. A new girl came to our school later and was accepted into the popular clique. She ended up seriously dating a guy from another grade level for a long time, and it ended rather ugly. There was a lot of anger, shame, bitterness and pain. She confessed afterwards that she had initially liked another guy, but she felt she was not good enough for him.

She settled. She limited herself to her false perception of who she was, and wound up really hurt.

Since then, I've met so many people with that same internal lie: "I am not good enough."

Whether it's good enough to date someone, good enough to go to college, good enough to play a sport, good enough to cook nice meals for your family, good enough for that job or good enough for anything else, so many people believe the lie that they are not good enough.

Do you believe this lie? Examine yourself. Stop and think. What dreams did you have when you were young? Do you still have that same amazing dream? Has someone told you that you are not good enough to do it? Have you replaced it with something much smaller because you bought into the lie that you are not good enough?

I knew about a family of five kids, and nearly all of them believed they were dumb and would not amount to much. One eventually graduated from college. She refused to believe the lie that she was not smart enough to be successful-even when one of her teachers told her she'd never graduate.

Speaking of teachers. Most are good people. Some are not (like the aforementioned one). One of the most heartbreaking things teachers regularly see is young students who already believe lies about themselves and their potential.

Having taught thousands of middle schoolers, I know two things to be true. First, some parents are amazing. These are the parents that are involved and generally love their kids. They realize having children means they have to give up some of themselves and reprioritize certain things to raise their children well.

Second, some parents suck! I mean some people should not be allowed to be responsible for other human beings. Period. In order to drive a car in most states, you must pass a paper test to get a learner's permit, have it for at least six months and then pass a road test. But anybody can have a child and raise that human almost however he or she sees fit.

Ok, back from that rabbit trail.

How is it that so many 11 year old children believe such limiting lies about themselves? Who told them they can't go to college? Who told them they will never be a good artist? Who told them they will never be good at math or science or reading or social studies? It's tragic. That word is overused, but when young kids believe such negative ideas about themselves, it is, indeed, *tragic*.

And what is worse is that without some kind of significant intervention, these children grow into adults believing a lie that dictates how they behave, who they talk to and what opportunities they pursue or choose not to pursue.

89

However, the thing about lies is that you do not have to believe them. People will lie to you. Society will lie to you. Friends and family might lie to you. You don't have to lie to yourself.

In Collegedale, TN, there is a memorial to an American hero who fought in WWII. This hero never carried a gun or recorded a kill. Others told him repeatedly that he was a liability, a distraction, a sorry excuse of a soldier and worse. Not only was he literally fighting "The War to End All Wars," he was also fighting a psychological war. Despite the verbal attacks, he kept encouraging himself.

Desmond Doss joined the army as a conscientious objector in 1942. Refusing to carry a gun for religious beliefs, he signed up to be a medic. He planned to save life instead of taking it. His refusal to carry a gun caused more than a minor issue with his fellow soldiers and officers who would refer to him as a disgrace, a coward and a traitor.

Desmond kept hearing the lies over and over. When he would start to believe them, he would encourage himself. He would speak positively over himself. He would remind himself of his purpose. He would pray. He refused to believe lies that so many others spoke over himself so often.

And because he refused to believe the lies, U.S. Army Private First Class Desmond Doss literally became an American hero. On May 5, 1945, in some of the bloodiest fighting of the war on Hacksaw Ridge in Okinawa, Doss stayed behind pulling wounded soldier after wounded soldier to safety. He is credited with single-handedly saving the lives of 75 soldiers in one night! A few months later President Truman presented Doss with the Medal of Honor. Doss also received the Purple Heart, the Bronze Star of Valor and a number of other awards for his service in the Pacific.

Doss did not believe the lies, and you don't have to either.

Summary

When we are young, we receive hundreds, perhaps thousands, of messages on a daily basis. Some messages are positive while others are negative. Each person receives a different amount of positive versus negative messages. One of the greatest factors that affects one's future are the messages he or she believes to be true. Unfortunately, negative messages sent to us repeatedly or under certain circumstances can take root and grow in our hearts and minds, often without us even being aware of them. Are there any lies that you believe about yourself? Have you ever set limitations for yourself? If so, why? The good news is that internal lies we believe can be broken. You can leave them in the past and get a fresh start. The first step is recognizing them. Begin reaffirming the truth in your life. Seek counseling if need be. Restore hope in your life, and begin to dream again.

Let me leave you with these powerful lyrics from someone who I think is one of the greatest songwriters ever, NF:

"Everybody's got a blank page

A story they're writing today

A wall that they're climbing

You can carry the past on your shoulders

Or you could start over."[1]

"We find comfort among those who agree with us - growth among those who don't."

— Frank A. Clark

Chapter 13
They are bad people.

This is one of those lies of which most people are completely unaware. Unfortunately, our society has evolved in such a way that instead of proving one thing right based on logic, observation and merit, people often demonize and criticize the other side to the extent that your subconscious perspective buys into the lie that those who are different in a particular way are bad. This is perhaps nowhere more noticeable than when it comes to certain people groups. You believe that *they* are bad people, even though you never actually came to that conclusion through unbiased reason or intentional thoughtfulness. It is a message you received throughout much of your life, sometimes from the media you consume and sometimes from loved ones. Often, it is the belief of those you respect and look up to. Many of us have an ingrained understanding that certain groups of people are bad.

And *they* can be a number of different people. *They* can be democrats, republicans, lawyers, homeless people, used car salesmen, Christians, Muslims, atheists, Jews, black people, white people, gay people, straight people, southerners, yankees, Asians, blue collar workers, Wall Street financial types, pro-mask during Covid people, anti-mask during Covid people, athletes, artsy people, etc. The list goes on and on. I can't possibly cover all groups, and I am sure I am forgetting to name some of the most unfairly criticized groups. Let's focus on a few specifically.

It is common for republicans to assume democrats are bad, and common for democrats to assume the same about republicans. Republicans accuse democrats of spending too much, growing the government too big, being too liberal and taking away your freedom. Democrats accuse republicans of neglecting the poor, favoring the rich, being too conservative, and being racist.

Here's a mind-blowing fact: not all democrats nor all republicans are bad. Actually, I believe the opposite is closer to the truth. There are both many good democrats and many good republicans.

I have another observation that I want to share with you. In my experience, a great number of people have the largest blind biases when it comes to their political stance.

This became extremely clear to me after a number of political conversations I have had over the years. Some of these conversations meandered for ridiculously stupid lengths of time and went absolutely nowhere.

Then, I remembered my philosophy class in college when we debated why some people will stand by their side regardless of all reason and evidence to the contrary. I must admit that at the time, I thought this point in the lesson was ridiculous. I mean who would be shown irrefutable evidence that they were wrong and still argue their position? Who does that?!

"No one except crazy people," I thought.

Then, I went out into the real world. I became an adult, began to pay my bills, went to work, hung out with friends and discussed some of the bigger things in life. The topic of politics often comes up. I soon understood why many people avoid the subject altogether...because some people are indeed crazy! Others are flat out unreasonable in this area.

I eventually realized there was one sure fire way to tell if someone was hopelessly blinded by their politics. If they were a republican, I would ask them to say one good thing about Obama or one bad thing about Bush. If they were a democrat, I asked them the opposite: to say one good thing about Bush or one bad thing about Obama.

If they couldn't, then I knew the conversation was pointless. (You can try with more recent presidents if you want to use this litmus test.)

Yes, I have my own biases, as well. But being aware of your biases is the first step to overcoming them.

No person is perfect. Every president has made good decisions and poor decisions. If someone is interested in politics and informed of the news, then they cannot observe four flawless or four completely flawed term years. It's just not possible. Therefore, if they are unable, or unwilling, to admit just one point that goes against their biases, then not only is the conversation moot, but also that person has bought into the lie that *they* are bad people.

What about you? Can you admit something negative about your political party? Or something positive about the other?

Hmmmmm...

What is frightening is that the media pushes extremely biased agendas. In my attempts to get a more neutral view of the world, I check both CNN and Fox News regularly. There's rarely a positive story about Republicans on CNN or positive story about Democrats on Fox. Half of what both report seems to be nothing more than "fake news."

The regular onslaught of political, irrational, biased perspectives of the opposition as *bad* people is extremely dangerous. It's like a disease that can spread into so many areas of our lives. It often drives the way we view rich people and poor people. It fuels the way people think about taxes. It affects how people feel about immigration. Should we raise taxes or lower them? Why do people pay different percentages? What percent of Americans should pay income tax? Should we have a larger or smaller government? How much control should the government be allowed? How far does free speech go? What about freedom of religion... or my freedom from your religion? How about masks during Covid?

Here are some statements you may have heard people share that reveal their bias. I'm paraphrasing, but you'll get the gist...

"Greedy rich people are why this country is falling apart."

"The CEOs are the people who drive our economy, support millions of working Americans and keep the costs of goods down."

"Homeless (or poor) people are just lazy! They'd rather mooch off society than get a job."

"The homeless are victims of our society and it's broken system. They just need some help and support to get back on their feet."

"We need a border wall to keep out the illegals."

"It's racist to build a wall; the only reason to build a wall is to keep people in need out."

[Rabbit Trail: Immigration and helping others is an extremely important and complex issue. Most people are not aware there is

96

basically a neon billboard sign at the edge of our country which reads, "Give me your tired, your poor, your huddled masses yearning to breathe free."[1] We have indeed invited "the wretched refuse" (probably not a very politically correct phrase anymore). However, as witnessed in sanctuary cities across the country, there is a tipping point at which the people are too numerous to be supported by the local resources like housing, education, employment, etc. There needs to be a balance, and there is not a simple answer.]

"Rich people need to pay more taxes."

"Everyone should pay the same percent."

"This country was founded on religion!"

"This country was founded so people could be free from oppressive religion." "People who refuse to wear masks are killing people!"

"People demanding everyone wear a mask are control freaks and un-American!"

Can you see the irrational extremes people jump to when it comes to their politics? *They* are not bad people. Please help stop that lie.

In fact there are two simple things I think we all can do to slow political hate speech. First, instead of spewing hate at why liberals or conservatives are "the devil," maybe share why your political ideas have merit and offer a reasonable solution to the problem. Second, when you see an irrational headline on the news or post on social media, just ignore it and move on. The fewer clicks and responses, the quicker it goes away.

Next, there's religion. Everyone has likely heard some family member suggest never to speak of politics or religion. Well, we already discussed one, so why not get our hands dirty with the other?

After 9/11, Islam was probably the most hated religion in the country. Then about a decade later, something unexpected happened. After a number of attacks on Muslims (and Muslim-looking people in America) following September 11th, the pendulum swung from anger and hate toward sympathy for the way many Americans viewed Muslims.

Islam claims to be a religion of peace. There are also extremists. To say all Muslims are terrorists is ignorant. To say all Muslims are good people is also a denial of reality.

Jews are said to be the most persecuted people in history, and that's hard to argue if one studies the history. It also feels they are one of the most divisive people groups, not because they want to be, but because others seem to love or hate them. It seems like people either want them dead or want to kill anyone who wants them dead. If you stop and think about this for long, you're in real danger of finding your self depressed...or in a rage.

Christians are said to be hypocrites, greedy, close-minded, prideful and "holier than thou." Christians are also the reason many homeless people get fed daily and have a place to sleep on frigid nights, responsible for building thousands of hospitals across the globe (especially in areas of need), provide millions of Christmas gifts for those less fortunate and have major outreach programs all over the world.

Interestingly enough, all three of these aforementioned religions all claim at least one historic Patriarch: Abraham. Jews and

Muslims claim a different inheritance through his two sons, Ishmael and Isaac. Christians side with Jews here, but then branch off around 2,000 years ago with Jesus of Nazareth, who they recognize as the Messiah.

Then there are atheists and agnostics. These folks don't particularly care for the worship of any God, or god, unless of course it is themselves. Not that they actually worship themselves in a religious sense, but by not having anyone else to worship, then they become their own gods by default–they have absolute power to make all their own decisions without any standard or accountability except that which they create themselves.

There are other religions, but these four major worldviews cover the large majority of those in the United States. With this understanding, I encourage you not to label any of these people groups as "bad people." Do each of them have some bad apples? Sure. But it is also true that people have inherent value. People have freedom to make good choices and to give hope, encouragement and love to others.

I am not suggesting that they are all the same. In fact, there are major differences in each. There should be easy to understand core values of each of these worldviews. Also, actions speak louder than words. What evidence do you see from these worldviews? What seeds are planted? What fruit is produced? Who is most active serving at the homeless shelter in your town? Please don't take one bad apple you remember in school or at your workplace and make a blanket statement on an entire group of people.

Some people have labeled certain minority groups as *bad*. Some people of color have labeled white people as *bad*.

To either of these, I just want to say, "Really?!"

If this is you, it is time to get to *know* some more people that don't look like you. Don't just know their name, where they work and how many kids they have, but know who they are, what they enjoy, what worries them and what dreams they have.

Lawyers are often given a bad rap for being greedy and conniving. This is likely true for some. Some lawyers were indeed responsible for prolonging segregation, keeping bad people out of jail and sending other innocent people to jail. However, many lawyers have worked long and hard, and often at much lower rates of pay, to fight injustice, stop discrimination, protect vulnerable people, and bring positive change in times of need and uncertainty.

I remember a funny story I heard a long time ago about a governor who was asked about what he could do to improve the quality of the nefarious population at the state pen, to which he promptly replied, "We can start incarcerating law abiding citizens!"

His logic was simple: if you put all the worst people in the state under one roof, of course, the population will not behave like angels. Sometimes, there's an easy explanation to the absurdity of some of our biases.

Who do you think are *bad* people and how did you arrive at the conclusion? Could your reasoning be flawed? How might the world change if you and others refused to label them, or anyone else, as bad people anymore?

<u>Summary</u>

Bias is something that we often see so clearly in others yet can be so difficult to recognize in ourselves. Our society has become very polarizing causing many of us to label others as *bad* people. Maybe we
100

are scared of those who are different. Maybe we are so desperate to be right. Maybe our family and friends all believe a certain way. Maybe we had a bad experience with a person or small group of people from a specific demographic. Maybe, you've just grown up sheltered or unfamiliar with a certain group of people. Whatever the reason, I challenge you to quit believing the lie now that they are *bad* people. I challenge you to extend more grace to those who are different.

"There are two opinions in this world: those who are right and everyone else who is not me."

— my college professor

Chapter 14
Everyone is so biased (except me).

"It's so difficult to understand you," the Zimbabwean kindergarten teacher expressed to me through her thick South African accent.

I slowly replied acknowledging that I understood our accents were very different.

"Yes," she said and then continued with mild exasperation, "But at least when I speak, you can clearly understand what I am saying." The headmaster and I glanced at each other before an amusing smile began to show on our faces.

"No, dear," the headmaster, with an accent of her own, kindly said to the teacher, "He has just as much trouble understanding you as you do him."

The teacher's chin dropped a bit as she slowly realized we both had the same challenge. She wasn't arrogant. She wasn't unkind. Like all of us, she simply had an understanding of the world from her perspective and her own experiences. At that moment, she had another experience, she accepted it and grew as a person.

Bias is difficult to define concisely, but it basically is a prejudicial perspective for or against something. Often, most people are not even aware they have bias in certain areas; this is referred to as unconscious bias. Most biases are rather harmless like how a food tastes, a favorite movie, a scent one dislikes, or even whether or not one thinks an accent is understandable. However, like the previous chapter revealed, it's the deeper, more serious biases such as those based on race, religion, politics and culture that can be very dangerous.

A while ago, I posted about a humbling, painful experience in which my bias about the limits of my body given my age became undeniably apparent, not only to myself, but to all those around me.

I titled it *Confessions of a Middle-Aged Church League Softball Player*, and here's a piece *of* it:

I'm old. It's official. I can no longer deny it (like my older brother). It happens at different times in different places for different folks. For me, it occurred 54 days before my 40th birthday about half way between 3rd base and home. At the direction of the 3rd base coach/pastor yelling, "Go! Hard!" I went. Hard. And in mid-sprint, pop! I stopped. I didn't know what hit me. But in the adrenaline of the moment, I immediately stepped forward again...and nearly fell over. And again. One more stop. One more step. Repeat. I wasn't sure what was happening, but three things were crystal clear: one, home plate was so close that I could see the cleat marks on it. Two, I couldn't put any weight whatsoever on my left leg to get me there. And three, I'd make an excellent extra in the next zombie movie. I was hamstrung (pun intended if wish-sorry, dad jokes come naturally to me b/c I'm a...well, you get it).

I should have seen this coming...if for no other reason than the fact that the running lame joke on the team was about who was going to sprain an ankle, pull a hamstring or otherwise hobble off the field next. Apparently, a couple years earlier on the church's first team, four men succumbed to similar injuries. Despite the constant comments on the text thread or in the dugout, it never really occurred to me that I had any real chance to get an injury. That stuff happens to, well, old dudes. (Upon further reflection, it has since occurred to me that about five of my teammates are technically young enough to be my children.)

The evidence surrounded me: all 39 birthdays, my children who were learning to drive, the old guy jokes, the gray hair that mocked me in the mirror, the comments about my still playing sports "at your age," the other guys (even 10 years younger) who had gotten injured and how long many of these guys would stretch just because they might run a couple times around the bases.

It didn't matter. I was invincible. I was a proud athlete who never had a major injury beyond sprained ankles that kept me sidelined for a couple months.

I think Blaise Pascal was speaking on a deeper level than overconfident athleticism when he said, "People almost invariably arrive at their beliefs not on the basis of proof but on the basis of what they find attractive."

That quote rings true for all biases, no matter how great or small. We tend to believe what we are taught, what we learn from experience, what we find attractive, and what our families and close friends believe.

Everyone has bias. Both me and you.

To say you have no biases is to live in denial.

But there is hope.

"Fortunately for serious minds," said painter Benjamin Haydon, "a bias recognized is a bias sterilized."

This works two ways. First, when you recognize bias in others or in the media, you can take what they are sharing with a grain of salt. Second, when you recognize a bias within yourself (and this is much more challenging), you can then pause, reflect and start trying to reconsider the validity of your position.

To deny you have bias is to lie to yourself and deny yourself truth. To recognize you have bias gives you the opportunity to grow and be a better person. Just because you have a bias does not mean you are wrong. Often, we have biases that are true. On the other hand, statistically, it's virtually impossible for all of one's biases to be true, so we all need to reexamine our biases when we recognize them.

Summary

I think this is the shortest chapter in the book, and that's because it's pretty straightforward. Everyone has bias. No one wants to be wrong. We're all human. We all have a desire to be right and "win the argument." This is natural. The real danger and the real damage, however, can come when our biases blind us to the truth. Some biases are rather harmless. Other biases, particularly those that become prejudices towards people groups, are downright ugly, create dissention, make people feel worthless, stir hate and can lead to all kinds of nastiness. As people in the 21st century, we have to be better than this. Be conscious of your biases. Recognize that you might be wrong. It's okay; we're all wrong sometimes. If you realize that your bias has hurt someone else, apologize. Look them in the eye, and say you're sorry. This is how you grow, and if you can help someone else grow alongside you, now you're in real danger of making the world a better place!

"Character is what you are in the dark."

- D. L. Moody

Chapter 15
What she doesn't know won't hurt her.

This is the classic lie that men tell themselves and other men, so they can do so-called harmless things that won't hurt the woman he "loves" because she won't know. I put quotations around *loves* in the previous sentence because logically there is a clear disconnect in truly loving someone and also living by this adage.

Before exploring the specifics, first let's recognize that this lie is not only told by men to women. Some women also use this same deceitful reasoning in romantic relationships. To a lesser extent, groups of friends, or even family members, will say this when they want others and themselves to feel less shame about leaving someone out or doing something behind one's back.

There are some other instances in which you'll hear the, "What she doesn't know..." lie, but for the purposes of this chapter, let's focus on this rationale in romantic relationships. That's where this lie is most often used, whether spoken verbally or a justification in one's mind, for doing something one knows he shouldn't.

Think about love. What does love mean to you? When you have children and they are grown, how do you want them to be loved?

So, can you love someone and practice the, "What she doesn't know, won't hurt her," mentality?

The short answer is, "No, not if you *really* love her."

There are many ways to define love, and if you search its definition online, you'll see a lot of common themes like affection, endearment, positive emotion, pleasure, passion, romance, devotion, etc. To be clear, we're specifically talking about romantic love and being in love, not my love of a juicy double cheeseburger.

In this context, love is a virtue. It has standards. For instance, my wife and I love each other; therefore, we are not going to have sex with anyone else. That's pretty simple to understand.

Your romantic love should be reserved for only one other person in your life; therefore, it is one of the rarest and greatest gifts you have to share. Think about it: you can only romantically love one person at a time, and when you find that person, you typically want to keep him or her for the rest of your life. Thus, love is perhaps the highest gift you can give and should also have some of the highest standards to protect and nurture it.

Love is *not* selfish. Love is selfless. Love is giving and serving; it is not merely seeking to receive. Love comes hand-in-hand with other values like respect, kindness, honesty and sacrifice. If the relationship you are in doesn't have these other values, then you're not in love.

Yeah, I just said that. If I offended you, I kinda feel sorry, but not really. I care about you enough to tell you the truth, even if it hurts.

If you disagree, stay with me for a minute. Think about all the people in all the relationships you know. Think of the good relationships. Now, think of the bad ones. Of these relationships that you know, have you seen any examples of relationships that you 100% don't want your future relationships to look like? Do you see any examples of relationships that you would love for your future relationships to model? What do those good relationships have in common?

Respect. Trust. Kindness. Generosity. Care. In a word, *love*.

Now that we've established a better understanding of true, romantic love, it's much easier to see why you can't love someone and live by the mentality that, "What she doesn't know won't hurt her."

The truth is that loving someone is not just being kind, showing passion, feeling butterflies in your stomach, and sacrificing, but love also involves honesty, trust and devotion. This is why what she doesn't know will indeed hurt her. When you are hiding things, complete honesty is lacking. When you are not fully honest, you don't have total trust.

First of all, she will likely be harmed twice when she learns of your deception. She is harmed once by what you hid and then secondly by your deception. Most things eventually come out. Christians refer to this as reaping what you sow. Buddhists and Hindus call it karma. Others might refer to it as a natural flow in the universe. Regardless, the principle of lies being revealed or consequences for your actions has been observed, taught and accepted by billions of people over hundreds of generations.

Secondly, even if she never finds out, there is harm because you are not fully giving yourself to her in love. When you love someone, do you want the other person to be all in? Most people would say, "Yes."

However, if you are holding things back, particularly things that you feel your lover would be harmed just by knowing, you are not loving fully. You are putting hard limits on how much your love can grow. You might be giving part of yourself, but you're definitely not giving all of yourself. You are setting a very real boundary line of where the love stops, and when your relationship reaches this line, the other person will be hurt.

Thirdly, even if the secret is not revealed, she will be hurt the more she gets to know you and realizes you are hiding things from her. A natural part of being in love is getting to know someone better than anyone else in the world. This requires vulnerability. In a healthy relationship, the two of you will reach a point in which you know practically everything about each other including when the other is being completely honest and open and when the other has been deceptive.

Let's pause and follow a rabbit down the vulnerability trail real quickly. Often, men refer to other men who are vulnerable as *weak*, but in reality it is those men who can't or won't ever be vulnerable who are truly the weak ones. Now, there is a time and place. I'm not suggesting you be the man who spills his guts in front of a group of strangers for sympathy. That guy is immature and seeking attention. I'm referring to the man who won't even open up to his inner circle. That guy's weak. A real man has the courage to be honest and vulnerable to those few closest people in his life, and he grows stronger when he does.

In my opinion, I think the average man (or woman) who spreads this lie that what she doesn't know won't hurt her is not void of love. His love is just misplaced. He simply loves *himself* more than his woman. His desires are the most important thing to him. He likes the idea of being in love, but not the sacrifice. He does not want to be completely honest. He does not want to put her feelings above his desires. He doesn't respect her enough not to do what he knows will hurt her. He wants to have his cake and eat it too. He loves himself more than her. She'll eventually realize this. And when she does, how long will she stay, and if she stays, how much of her heart will she start holding back?

Summary

People are selfish. We see selfishness all over our society. One of the few places where selfishness should be absent is in a loving, romantic relationship; however, people (largely men) have been bringing selfishness into their relationships under the guise of, "What she doesn't know won't hurt her." Often, people are using this to justify doing or viewing something they should not. This is a dangerous lie. It tries to communicate innocence and a victim-less mentality, so one can continue to do what he desires without guilt. However, the truth is not only does it often harm the victim, but it also prevents the person who spreads this lie from maturing into a person who can have a healthy, completely in-love relationship. The truth is that deception and dishonesty are harmful and have no place in lasting, romantic relationships. If you want to live your life a certain way that would harm your romantic partner, then *don't get involved*. Stay single. Don't be a selfish jerk. If you find yourself falling in love or want to be in a healthy relationship, then MAN UP and quit negative behaviors that will harm her. The truth is that being in love requires honesty, sacrifice and change, and it is worth every bit of it! It's awesome! But start becoming that person now, so you don't miss out on her later. The good ones are not common.

"Half of the troubles of this life can be traced to saying yes too quickly and not saying no soon enough."

—Josh Billings

Chapter 16
Yes.

Have you ever seen a parent tell a *spoiled* child, "No," to something he really wants?

"Pleasant" is likely not the word most would use to describe the ensuing madness.

The bright red face. The quivering lip. The crying. The screaming. The flailing. The stomping. The hands on the hips. The anger in the eyes. But wait, there's more…Then comes the wailing pleas stacked with layers of guilt.

"You don't love me!"

"I never get anything I want!"

"You never do anything for me!"

"I wish I were dead!"

"If you ever loved me, you'd let me have this one thing! It's all I've ever wanted!"

The list goes on.

Unfortunately, we've all seen this reaction from spoiled children. It seems to be more common at home with familiar people around. Sometimes, it happens in public at the store, playground, ball game or wherever.

As a teacher and father of six who has attended countless children's events, I've witnessed these tantrums from pretty much every demographic: white, minority, rich, poor, urban, rural, white-collar, blue-collar, biological, and blended families. The sight never gets better. It's always one of the most irritating, uncomfortable and disturbing family scenes to observe.

Sometimes, the parents stick to their original, "No." However, many times for whatever reason, the parents relent and give in completely or make some kind of compromise to pacify the child.

In my opinion, this is the worst thing that can happen for the child. Instead of teaching children that "No," is the answer for some things, the child's irate behavior is rewarded and reinforced. This pattern undermines children hearing, "No," as a perfectly legitimate and acceptable answer.

Sadly, some people never mature to the point of being able to control themselves when told, "No." That's why physical and mental abuse, theft, rape, road rage, couples screaming at each other in public, people quitting jobs abruptly in a rage and other similar outbursts in adults are so common in our society.

Thankfully, most people eventually mature out of their childhood emotional and violent fits, but not everyone. Many of us Americans, instead of accepting, "No," as an answer, tell ourselves–and others–"Yes," way too often. In this way, we can still have what we want. We relabel our *wants* as *needs* so we can justify having it now when we are not really in a good position to assume it.

We keep lying to ourselves, saying, "Yes," when what we really need to say is, "No," or, "Not now, but maybe later."

Think about it. As Americans, we live in the most materialistic society the world has ever seen, and we always want more.

For instance, the majority of Americans eat better than 90% of kings throughout history. The large majority of Americans eat meat every single day if they want. The large majority of Americans have access to fresh fruits and vegetables throughout the year. We enjoy candy bars, ice cream, pie, cake, cookies and other sweets all year long. I don't know how many pounds of sugar and corn syrup are consumed over our holidays, but my guess is it's in the millions. One final thought to consider: most Americans can order just about any type of food in the world from their phone or computer and have it delivered or "dashed" to them within an hour.

It's not just food. How many people do you know that take multiple vacations or getaways every year? Many of these people are either in debt or have zero savings. We can order nearly any product imaginable and have it shipped to our house within two days or within hours if we are willing to pay the delivery fee. The cost of college has skyrocketed because we want our children to go to a school that has an Olympic size swimming pool, a variety of brand-name restaurants to choose from in the cafe, a great outdoor and leisure program, the newest academic buildings, state of the art workout facilities, and top-notch sports teams. (Now we're paying these once "amateur" athletes millions of dollars, but that's another story.) Many people are willingly paying hundreds of dollars for a pair of shoes. Christmas has become a commercial competition on who can buy the most and get the most. It just doesn't end.

I know a family who was struggling financially. The man was perpetually "between jobs." He was also behind on child support. His wife hadn't worked for a while so she could take care of the kids. Then one day, she finally got a job. She quickly had a vehicle that is much more expensive than the one either my spouse or I (whose income is considerably more) drive. Then they received some extra money. Most of it went to excessive Christmas gifts for their kids. Needless to say, after a year or so, they're struggling financially more than ever. Whenever they have money, they tell themselves, "Yes," to whatever they want.

When it comes to being told, "No," two stories about my favorite athlete, Michael Jordan, come to mind. The first story is well-known, and coaches across the country use it regularly to motivate potential players. As a high school sophomore, Michael was cut from his high school basketball team. He was told, "No," and didn't make his high school basketball team when he was in the tenth grade. In response, Michael practiced harder than he had ever before. He made himself better and stronger. The rest is history; Michael Jordan won 6 NBA championships and is considered by many the G.O.A.T of basketball.

It's interesting to consider what would have happened if Michael had gone to his coach crying, and his coach had let him on the varsity team that year. Would his work ethic have become what it did? Would his drive to perfect his game have been as great? Without that defining moment of motivation, would he still have become one of the most famous people in the world? We may never know, but fortunately his coach didn't lie to him and tell him, "Yes," when he did not yet deserve to be on the team.

The other story is more obscure, took place nearly four decades later and involves Jordan's former friend Charles Barkley.

Barkley is definitely not my favorite athlete. In fact, he's done a lot of things that are rather foolish in my opinion; however, I respect Barkley for a variety of reasons. For one, he was probably the best out-of-shape athlete I have ever seen. That's not an insult; it's legit. Virtually every other athlete with that level of success had to spend hours upon hours of conditioning and working out, but Barkley played with a fierceness, drive and intelligence that made up for it. Also, he is one of the best basketball minds when it comes to analyzing players and the game. Finally, he is brutally honest. He will not tell you what you want to hear. He respects himself enough and you enough to tell you the truth, even if he knows you will disagree.

I have followed both Michael and Barkley closely since I started collecting their basketball cards around 1990. They played on the Dream Team together in 1992 winning gold in Barcelona and then competed for the NBA championship the next season. They were good friends for the next thirtyish years. Then they had a falling out.

In an interview with 60 Minutes, Charles Barkley was asked about why he and Michael Jordan stopped talking. Barkley responded by explaining that he told Michael, "that he don't have enough people around him that gonna tell him, 'No,' and he got really offended and we haven't spoken."[1]

I have no idea how that conversation between Jordan and Barkley really played out or who's to blame and what else was said, etc.

But what I do know is that Barkley's statement about not having enough people around that will tell you, "No," is all too true for many of us. It's easy and convenient to surround ourselves only with people who will support us, even if we're not making the best decisions. No one likes to be told, "No." That is literally *denying ourselves* of what we want. Of course, you're not going to embrace it, but you need to accept it when it's legit.

As an adult, I have witnessed one of the people closest to me cut a half dozen people or so out of her life, all because they either disagreed with her or told her, "No." Regrettably, I have known a number of others like her.

Eliminating people who tell you, "No," when it's in your best interest is dangerous. It creates an environment in which you'll never be seriously challenged when you're about to do something negative. Nobody's perfect. We all make mistakes, so having only "yes people" in your life won't prevent you from making bad decisions.

I think there's too many people in our society that live like this. We want to do what we want, and we don't want people to tell us, "No." But, we have to quit lying to ourselves and having others lie to us by saying, "Yes," to poor choices.

Earlier, I mentioned a friend who told me to stop reaching out to him if I was going to continue in my foolishness. He was in my wedding, and I consider him one of my best friends to this day. He, my wife, brother, parents and about five other guys, can tell me, "No," and I will listen. I know they have my best interest in mind, so I value their opinions, even when, or especially when, they disagree with me. It causes me to self-reflect, and often I follow their advice.

Here's one final point.

CNBC released an article saying that 60% of Americans live paycheck to paycheck.[2] Some say that America is the wealthiest, most prosperous country ever. Some people might disagree, so let's just say it's at or nearly the wealthiest country in the world right now. The majority of the population has nothing saved for later, for a downpayment on a house, for retirement, for their kids' college education. Why are so many people in such a prosperous nation so financially vulnerable?

I think this is directly related to people saying, "Yes," to whatever they want and refusing to tell themselves, "No." They keep lying to themselves, saying that they can do this or that.

The truth can be hard. The truth can hurt.

There is a concept of delayed gratification, which is saying, "No," to something now, so you can say, "Yes," to something else later. A man might drive a "beater" for a couple years, so he can save up and buy a newer vehicle with cash as opposed to financing a new car. A college student may limit her social time so she can work 15 hours a week in college so she can graduate debt free. A young lady might refuse to have sex with a guy until a certain time period (like number of dates or, dare I suggest, marriage) because she doesn't want certain risks unless she knows something is real. A guy might be willing to agree to her standards because he knows *she* is the kind of woman he wants to spend the rest of his life with and raise his children. These are examples of delayed gratification.

Summary

You are not perfect and right about everything; therefore, telling yourself, "Yes," to every feeling or desire you have is essentially lying to yourself. The truth is that sometimes, we all need to be told, "No." Surrounding yourself with people who support you no matter how crazy you're acting is unhealthy. You need to have people in your life that are strong enough and care about you enough to speak truth into you, even when you might not agree. You are no longer a child, and even children need to learn when, "No," is appropriate. You are mature enough to delay gratification. Say, "No," to some things now so that later, you will have the freedom to say, "Yes." And who knows? At that point, you might have grown to the point where you don't even still want that frivolous thing anyway.

"A well-supported evidence-based theory becomes acceptable until disproved. It never evolves to a fact, and that's a fact."

—Tim Lewis (surgeon, professor and pathologist)

Chapter 17
You can't argue with science.

Haven't we all heard this before? Two people, or sometimes a group of people, will be in a heated debate over something. Shots are fired back and forth as each new idea is met with a sound rebuttal. As you're listening, you have an opinion, but you're unsure–perhaps, intimidated by the educated concepts and responses of people whose intelligence you respect–so you just wait.

Then, one of the "smart people" says, "Well, it's a scientific fact that…"

They make their point, and boom, the conversation's over. It might not end immediately, but people begin to back off on their passionate responses. The voice levels start going down, and before long, they move on to another subject or activity.

When people pull the, "You can't argue with science," card, it is dangerous on so many levels.

First of all, our society has a great misunderstanding of science and the term "scientific fact." Many people, perhaps most people, think scientific research is a perfect art with a mystic undeniability and anyone who disagrees with it is a bone-headed moron. That can't be further from the truth.

To start with, there is no such thing as scientific fact in the sense of what the common person considers fact. The common person considers a fact something concrete, something that never changes–ever. That's pretty much the definition of a fact.

In science, the term fact is more fluid.

The National Center for Science Education phrases it like this: "**Fact:** In science, an observation that has been repeatedly confirmed and for all practical purposes is accepted as 'true.' Truth in science, however, is never final and what is accepted as a fact today may be modified or even discarded tomorrow."[1]

Wow! If that doesn't give you pause in the certainty of scientific fact, I don't know what will. No, scientific facts are not constantly changing, but it's also not uncommon for scientific facts to change.

Secondly, scientific study encourages questioning the natural world and is supposed to have a healthy dose of skepticism.

But don't take it from me. A widely distributed middle school science textbook phrases it like this: "Scientists need to be open-minded, or capable of accepting new and different ideas. But open-mindedness should always be balanced with skepticism…"[2] The text then covered three different types of bias, honesty, ethics, objective reasoning, subjective reasoning and faulty reasoning over the next few pages.

Good science just doesn't accept something because it came from a science magazine, but it will check the conclusions with current understanding and observations to determine how valid a conclusion is.

Regular people do this naturally all the time. My parents and I are fortunate enough to live in the same town and see each other a couple times a month. My dad still reads a newspaper and watches the news almost daily, and like other senior citizens, one of his favorite topics is the weather. When I let him know I'm doing this or that, he often tells me that it's supposed to rain. So what do I do? I look out the window. I also check my phone for the latest forecast. Even though he reads the newspaper and watches the news, I don't take everything he says as 100% fact. I then decide whether I will continue with my plans or adjust them accordingly.

People regularly go through the scientific method to form conclusions and make decisions all the time. For example, last week I went to my softball game because it had not been delayed in spite of a chance of rain. I got on first, and then the game was called. As the officials received more data points (particularly the flash of lightning and clap of thunder), they formed a new conclusion that conditions were safe to play.

And the next time you hear someone say, "It's a scientific fact that…" it's okay to ask questions. Perhaps, what they are saying is perfectly legit. However, if what they are saying sounds suspect, you can challenge those conclusions. Respectful debate and disagreement can be–actually, should be–productive. They might learn something. You might learn something. Questions, observations and tests confirm many scientific theories. They also shine light on theories that are not so reliable, or in some cases, are flat out wrong.

Thirdly, science and scientific theory have a long history of changing, evolving and proving former theories and facts to be completely false. The scientific community used to know that the world was flat, Piltdown Man was a missing link, the night parrot had gone extinct, a planet named Vulcan existed, bloodletting was the cure for a variety of ailments, and the Earth was the center of the universe. More recent observations, experiments and explanations have since proven these and countless other "scientific facts" to be false.

Fourthly, people regularly misquote statistics and information or apply information illogically or incorrectly. Minor changes in wording can create very different outcomes. Also, when people are trying to prove their point and often don't fully understand what they are arguing, they pull a random quote from a scientist or lean on a statistic from somewhere, usually social media (my eyes are rolling as I type this) that seems to agree with their argument. Then, they follow it up by saying that it's scientifically researched and you can't argue with science.

However, if what someone is saying is an indeed scientifically sound argument, he should be able to explain the science so that others understand the reasoning rather than hiding behind the quote or statistic. Often there are variables that affect statistics or scientific beliefs. For instance, it was widely held that decaying meat produced maggots; afterall, this had been repeatedly observed by pretty much everyone for centuries until Francesco Redi's experiments in 1668 when he put gauze on top of jars next to jars without gauze on top.

Next, as discussed earlier, people are biased. Scientists are not immune to personal bias. In fact, I would suggest that scientists are some of the most biased people on the planet. Some scientists are religious, which can be a bias. Some scientists are agnostic, which can be just as much of a bias. Many scientists have financial implications to their research which can create a need to have a major breakthrough. Many scientific studies are paid for by groups in which there is a major conflict of interest. Think medicine, oil companies, conservation groups, politics, sports gambling, vehicle safety, alcohol, tobacco, etc.

During the COVID pandemic, there was significantly little science at the beginning of how coronavirus began and how it spread, yet people and politicians were making major decisions based on the "science" that affected all areas of life from the economy to education to exercise to dining to mental health to travel. It became a political issue. Everyone, especially politicians, only quoted research that supported their agendas and ignored research that contradicted their opinions. People looked at the same "science," and drew two different conclusions. When the mandates abruptly ended, people were left confused and unsure of how to move forward. Were things safe or not? (Full disclosure, I have a family member who worked at NIH during this time.)

Sometimes, our scientific understanding is way off, and no one knows exactly why. In the world in which we live, I regularly visit the website goodnewsnetwork.org to help myself stay balanced. The title of an article I read the other day is "Analysis Shows We've Been Overestimating the Amount of Plastic in Oceans by 30x."[3] Wow! That's not a small discrepancy.

Pictures of fossilized coelacanth fish were common in science textbooks though the mid 20th century. These fish which had gone extinct over 60 million years ago were clearly a transitional species of fish that had developed supportive limbs to come out of the water and move on the ground. However, in 1938, when a five foot coelacanth was caught alive, this theory had to be reexamined. Today, there are at least two known living species, and the supportive limbs have only been observed for swimming.

127

Am I saying that since science has been wrong so many times in the past and since people are biased that you should just not believe anything? No, absolutely not.

What I am saying is that you should use common sense and logical reasoning in determining what makes sense and what needs more explanation. Sound science is a good way to make strong conclusions about our universe and ourselves. Reading, studying, observing, hypothesizing and experimenting are great ways to develop a rational understanding of how things work. However, it should be balanced with some skepticism and questioning.

Many times, people will say, "It's scientifically researched," and their argument is indeed good science with sound conclusions.

However, there are also many times–especially in today's society with cell phones and the internet–that people use faulty logic or will make claims based on "science" and they proudly end it with, "And you can't argue with science!"

Well, actually, you can.

Summary

Science is a good thing. Safer travel, better medicine, more efficient food production and countless other benefits are the results of good science. The scientific method is used to draw strong, reasoned conclusions about how the world works. However, people are not perfect. People have biases. Sometimes, one's education is lacking, or there has been misinformation. Variables often change outcomes of what would normally be expected. Some people just want to stand out, so they make astonishing statements. Regardless of the reason, people often make weak or false claims and then defend them in the name of "science." Use your head. Sometimes, their logic is good. Sometimes, not so much. Other times, it's okay to know that someone else is wrong, and you don't have to say anything. Often, it's not worth your time or energy arguing with ignorant or overly biased people.

"The world isn't fair, Calvin."

"I know Dad, but why isn't it ever unfair in my favor?"

—Bill Watterson (Calvin and Hobbes)

Chapter 18
Life is fair.

This is a belief that almost every young kid has. I'm not exactly sure where or how the concept of fairness begins in young children, but I'm confident every kid develops a concept of "fairness" early, as evidenced by how many times the words, "That's not fair!" are screamed at a playground, kids' birthday parties, on the ballfield, in the gym at school or a host of other activities.

Regardless of where fairness sits on *the nature vs. nurture* debate, it likely has a great deal of both. It seems that even children have a sense of right and wrong and fair or not before they can even speak. If you give a one year old child a treat but not the next kid at daycare, they seem to be aware that something is amiss. However, in daycare, kindergarten and often at home, teachers and parents often discuss fairness with children.

Then comes middle school. This seems to be where many children are first tangibly confronted with the concept that life isn't always fair. Whether it's getting cut from a team, having an easier math teacher or the whole class getting punished for the actions of a few, middle schoolers definitely hear and see *life not being fair* in action.

However, although people become very aware of this around the age of puberty, they seem to hold onto the idea of fairness. Fairness means that things are are equal. Things are just. Everyone should be treated the same. Everyone gets a trophy! (*oops, too far?*)

As we grow up and go through life, it seems that we have a set of expectations of how things should and should not be. When these expectations are unmet, disappointment and frustration are common. If these expectations were high, our reactions can pass from disappointment to anger, hurt, jealousy, fear, and other negative emotions. In extreme cases, they can lead to screaming, deep bitterness and even violence.

Why? Because of how highly we value fairness.

It's not wrong to value fairness. In fact, fairness is a positive thing and ought to be valued, but it should be balanced with the reality that life is not fair. I would also like to add the nuance that what is fair is not necessarily what is equal.

Gary Riggins, one of my graduate professors, said it like this: "There is nothing as unfair as the equal treatment of unequals."

Let that marinate a minute.

It took me months, well, probably a couple years of teaching to really grasp that. Should every student get the same consequence for the same behavior? Nope. Some students I can look at, and they will change their behavior. Others, I can walk by to redirect them. Others need me to speak directly to them. Still others will need a stern warning or an actual consequence to change their behavior.

Conversely, they all need different amounts of grace. Should a student raised by a married loving mom and dad be treated the same as a student in foster care who came from an abusive situation? Nope.

That said, I try to treat students as fairly as possible, especially when they're watching. But I'm not going to be as hard on the kid whose single mom didn't come home last night and had to feed his younger siblings as I am on the kid whose family has it together but just isn't prepared because he spends all his time on his new iPhone.

Nevertheless, our society keeps telling us that life is fair. Like I said, fairness is a positive thing. We should treat others fairly, but life itself is *not* fair and will not be fair to everyone. If we believe the lie that life is fair, we set ourselves up for disappointment, victim-mentality and failure.

Fairness is linked to comparison. If there is no comparison, then there can be nothing fair or unfair, it just is. When we compare, we are destined to fall short. When we are set on life being fair, we are setting ourselves up for disappointment.

Nothing is ever completely equal. Try breaking a cookie in half and splitting it between two young children. Parents know how that goes.

My wife and I have a blended family with six children. They make me proud. Sometimes, they drive me nuts. They are awesome. They are talented. They are gifted, and I love them.

But when it came to splitting desserts…yeah, there was never once we heard a chorus of, "Thank you!"s.

Instead we heard, "His is bigger!"

"Why did he get *that* piece?!"

"Yeah, that's because *she's* your favorite!"

"Why do I always get the smallest piece?"

So, you know what I learned to do? I will have one of them cut something in half, and have the other kid choose his piece. Of course, now no one wants to be the cutter!

I share that story, just to reiterate how nothing is perfectly fair.

133

You might have been raised in an abusive home, and your friends were not. Your neighbor might be rich, but you are not. Your friend got scholarships, but you had to take out loans. Your spouse has supportive parents, but you do not. Your co-worker's family is paying for his vacation to Hawaii, and you...well, probably not.

If you allow yourself to live in a reality that expects life to be fair, you are setting yourself up for failure and heartbreak. Life is not fair. Treat your friends, family and children with as much fairness as you can, but know that life will not always be fair to you, and that's okay.

Summary

Even though many Americans might admit that life is not fair, we still have a belief inside us that things ought to go a certain way, things ought to be fair. The more we hold on to this, the more disappointment, frustration, anger and victim-mentality will set in when life inevitably turns out to be unfair. I am not suggesting that you should be a walk over and never stick up for yourself. There will be a number of times when you need to draw a line, set a boundary and fight for what is right. However, there are many things outside your control that will benefit others more than you. Be careful not to compare their situations to yours. This only leads to negative feelings, and if left unchecked will lead to you living like you're a victim. Only you can live your life. The world is not against you, but life is tough. Life is not fair. It's easier to overcome any obstacle that comes your way when you tackle it head on, as opposed to whining about how unfair it is. Roll with the punches. YOU control your future!

134

"The faith that anyone could move from rags to riches – with enough guts and gumption, hard work and nose to the grindstone – was once at the core of the American Dream."

–Robert Reich, former U.S. Secretary of Labor

Chapter 19
The American Dream is Dead.

I was born in Tampa. My dad was born in Tampa. His dad, my grandpa, was born in Tampa and my grandma was born in New York. My great grandparents were born in Sicily.

In 2010 and in 2022, I was fortunate enough to visit Siracusa (Italy). Not only are my family roots there, but I still have cousins, removed a handful of times, who live there and took me to see the sights and family historical spots.

Around 1900, millions of people across the world immigrated to the United States. Among them were my great grandparents who had made the difficult decision to save enough money for a one way ticket in steerage class (google it) to New York.

The Statue of Liberty hadn't yet been erected to greet them when they arrived at Ellis Island, but they didn't need it. They had heard that America was the land of opportunity–that if you worked hard and made good choices, you could be successful, raise a family and lead a happy life.

The American Dream means different things to different people, but that is what it meant to my family and many others, and that is what they achieved.

There are a growing number of people, however, who say that the American Dream is dead. They rant and rail against capitalism, big business in America and our society. Others blame the United States government, its policies and the growing bureaucracy. Some aim their cynicism at both the government and big business.

Author Barbara Ehrenreich has written two New York Times bestselling books on the subject: *Nickel and Dimed: On (Not) Getting By in America* and *Bait and Switch: The (Futile) Pursuit of the American Dream.*[1,2] Each book was written after Ehrenreich did a personal social experiment. These social experiments lead to her conclusions.

[Or did they really...]

The subtitle of both books includes a (negative) description of life in America. You are welcome to read them, but I think both titles make pretty clear where her stance is on the American Dream and simply "getting by" or "(not) getting by" in this country.

Again, both of these books were New York Times bestsellers. That means there are at least thousands and thousands of these books in print. One has sold over two million copies! Additionally, they were required reading for a number of courses in colleges, universities and even some high schools across the country.

Why were they so successful? And why are people still eating up this perspective and negative type of reasoning?

If you're quiet enough, you can almost hear the whining...

"Life in America is too hard."

"Things were easier back then."

"I can't get a break."

"There are no good jobs available."

"The government is just holding the man down."

"I'm too stressed to devote 40 hours a week to a job." (I just threw up in my mouth a little bit.)

Whaaaaaaaaaaaaaa!

Arguing that the American Dream is dead is victim-mentality. It puts the blame for a person's shortcomings on society, government, education, big business or elsewhere instead of where it belongs–on the individual.

What if people quit blaming others and started putting the responsibility of their failure or success on their own shoulders, much like Americans have done for the past two and a half centuries?

Adam Shepherd read those two books and he resented Ehrenreich's conclusions so much that he went out, did his own personal social experiment and wrote his own book entitled *Scratch Beginnings: Me, $25, and the Search for the American Dream.*[3]

Shepherd explains his experiment best so I'll let him take over here:

"My story is a rebuttal to Barbara Ehrenreich's Nickel and Dimed and Bait and Switch, the books that spoke on the death of the American dream. With investigative projects of her own, Ehrenreich attempted to establish that working stiffs are doomed to live in the same disgraceful conditions forever. I reject that theory and my story is a search to evaluate if hard

137

work and discipline provide any payoff whatsoever, or if they are, as Ehrenreich suggests, futile pursuits."[3]

After starting out with only $25, a sleeping bag, a backpack and the clothes on his back but ending up with a furnished apartment, a truck, and over $5,000 in savings a year later, Shepherd concluded, "America is more fertile and full of more opportunity than any other country" and the American Dream is still very much alive.[3]

One theme I have repeated throughout this book is bias. It seems as if both Ehrenreich and Shepherd had preconceived notions about the American Dream. They also both found exactly what they were looking for. We need to be aware of our biases because they often determine how we view the world, the things we can accomplish and, sometimes more importantly, the things we cannot.

If after my family success story of the American Dream and reviewing the findings in *Scratch Beginnings: Me, $25, and the Search for the American Dream*, you are still toying with the lie that the American Dream is dead, let me share a sad but strong reality. Because of the freedom and opportunity for a better life, people are literally dying to get into our country. Exact statistics vary according to the source you choose, but in the past decade, thousands of people have died trying to get into the U.S. It's heartbreaking.

More positively, each year roughly two million people immigrate to the United States either legally or illegally.

Recently, a woman named Emily Francis came to speak at my school for in-service. She is one of the best speakers I've heard in years, and her story was captivating. Starting out in Guatemala selling oranges, her mother moved to New York as an undocumented person and left her around age 12 to watch her siblings (with help from the neighbors).[4] Many months later, her mother earned enough money to pay a coyote to take the siblings up to Mexico and eventually to New York. Lacking food, growing up in poverty, having to trust strangers, without consistent education as a small child, struggling through high school and facing more obstacles than most of us ever do, Emily struggled to overcome them to become a successful teacher, author and speaker.

(I don't condone or suggest doing what her mother did. I just want to share her story to communicate just how much some people believe in the American Dream and what they will do to have a chance to realize it.)

Summary

I'm not going to summarize this chapter. Instead, I'll just leave you with a few quotes.

"I was a poor kid. I came from nothing. We didn't have any money; a lot of times we didn't have any food, and now, all of a sudden, I'm a superhero in a Marvel movie? Talk about the American dream, man – I'm living it."—Dave Bautista

"I am the epitome of what the American Dream basically said. It said you could come from anywhere and be anything you want in this country."— Whoopi Goldberg

"I love entrepreneurship because that's what makes this country grow, and if I can help companies grow, I am creating jobs; I am setting foundations for future generations. It sends the message that the American Dream is alive and well."—Mark Cuban

Other people who have lived the American Dream are Oprah Winfrey, Arnold Schwarzenegger, Tyler Perry, Ben Carson, Sylvester Stallone, Elon Musk, Jeff Bezos and many successful people you know!

"I wouldn't be where I am now if I didn't fail, a lot. The good, the bad, it's all part of the success equation."

—Mark Cuban, billionaire and successful entrepreneur

"A calm sea never produced a good sailor."

Chapter 20
Successful people don't have real issues.

Long before the internet, YouTube, social media and on-demand TV, people had TVs. Shows came on at a certain time. If you were at practice, driving, cooking, working, outside, on the phone or in the restroom, you missed part or all of the show. I used to love watching *TGIF* (Thank Goodness It's Friday). Most of the shows were sitcoms–situational comedies–about quirky families, and in each episode there would be some silly issue that could be nicely and humorously resolved in 30 minutes, minus commercial breaks.

It was entertaining, but it wasn't reality.

In those sitcoms, people may have wrecked a car, broken a window, been set up with an ugly blind date, or had an embarrassing moment in front of their class, but those shows rarely addressed deep, real issues. You would never see shows with traumatic physical, sexual or emotional abuse. Contentious divorces and custody battles didn't make the line up. A family member suffering a slow, painful death from cancer was never a topic. Unwanted teenage pregnancies were not really addressed. The core members of the families never had a strong drug, alcohol, sex or gambling addiction. You never saw the family

141

driving the streets looking for a homeless family member who had mental health issues and would be gone for months at a time. The dad or mom never had an affair that broke up the family.

In short, most 1990s sitcoms were nice, clean family entertainment that touched on some minor things but never faced the uglier, messier side of humanity. Even if every episode didn't end with a hug and a smile, it at least ended with a warm, fuzzy feeling.

In my experience, there are many people today who seem to have the impression that successful people have that exact same type of life. If you listen to enough people or just scroll through social media, it has become clear that a growing number of Americans believe that successful people don't have real problems.

Over the past decade or so, I've had a rather wide range of experiences. I've been on the board of a nonprofit organization. I was a missionary and lived in Africa for over a year. I was divorced and remarried. I am a public school teacher. I have been through recovery and plugged in to at least three different national support groups for different hurts, habits and hangups. I play pickleball regularly with a local group. I have led small groups and served on a dream team at my church.

In short, I've met and spent a lot of time with many people from a large variety of backgrounds, and I have noticed a recurring belief in many people who are not satisfied with their lives. Most of them have bought into the lie that successful people have it easy. They think successful people have not had the real setbacks and obstacles that they have had to face. They think that the deck is stacked against them.

One guy I know talks nonstop about how our government is anti-dads when it comes to divorce and is always complaining about how much back child support he owes. He has had different jobs, and I know this is a constant financial battle for him.

On the other hand, I know a guy who contacted the child support office himself to have it taken directly from his paycheck, so he knew exactly how much he had to live on and then lives within his means on what's leftover.

I heard a lady talking about how she couldn't afford certain things that some of her friends were buying or doing. Later, I learned that this same lady was having her master bath remodeled because it was outdated. The bathroom was still functional, but the tile, paint and countertops were old. She chose to pay someone else nearly $20,000 to update her bathroom! Then if you listened to her talk, she felt like a victim because she couldn't afford the beach vacation she saw her friends enjoying on a school break.

Hmmmmm...

I have heard many people talking about how unfair it is that they know people whose parents are paying for school and they are having to get student loans, to work at college or doing both.

I have listened to a number of people talk about abuse and childhood trauma. I played softball with two men whose father's committed suicide when they were young. People close to me have struggled with addictions and depression. I know many people who have lost their parents, siblings and even children unexpectedly and at too young of an age. One particular family with four grown kids saw one son/brother attempt suicide and wind up with permanent brain damage and then the other brother successfully commit suicide weeks later. It was horrible. Others have been the victim of racism, sexism or harassment. In fact, the more I get to know people, the more I realize that *everyone* has issues.

Not all issues are equal, but *everyone* has real issues.

I've had many issues of my own, but I am thankful that I've been spared of many of the most traumatic. I didn't spend years in a concentration camp like Corrie Ten Boom nor was I ever a prisoner of war like Louis Zamperini. I wasn't born in jail before entering the foster care system and then subjected to years of abuse like Antwone Fisher. I wasn't born without limbs like Nick Vujicic or had a limb bitten off by a shark like Bethany Hamilton. I never was framed by a racist detective and served years in prison for a crime I didn't commit like Rubin Carter.

All these people have unfortunately faced trauma much greater than I have ever faced, and I listed each of them for a very specific reason. They all overcame their "issues." Ms. Boom went on to travel the world delivering a message of hope and forgiveness to hurting people. Mr. Zamperini, after struggling with alcohol, had a spiritual rebirth, forgave his torturers, founded a camp for troubled youth, and became an author. Mr. Fisher became a best-selling author and children's advocate. Mr. Vujicic overcame his condition also to be an actor, highly sought after motivational speaker, and also a best-selling author. Mrs. Hamilton returned to professional surfing, began writing inspirational books, had a family, and founded her own charitable outreach. Mr. Carter used his experience to advocate for others who were wrongfully accused and even became the executive director of the Association in Defense of the Wrongfully Convicted.

Not only did these successful people have real issues, but I would argue that it is because of these issues, that they became as strong and successful as they are. Without the trauma that they survived, they would likely not have had such a positive impact on humanity as they have had and we would likely not even know their names.

Everyone has issues. People who we view as successful and people who we view as unsuccessful all have challenges. Who they become is not determined by the trauma, drama, prejudice, abuse, hate or harm they experience but how they respond to it.

I'm not saying to not empathize with people who are hurt or going through stuff. People need love, support and encouragement. Some people need intense counseling over a period of years. Some people need to go through the stages of grief. Some people need time to cry and lick their wounds. Some people need mentors and friends who they have to lean on in the tough times. We all need something.

But what I am saying is that you can't get stuck. You can't believe the lie that because you've had issues, you can't be successful. You need to face those issues and deal with them appropriately. It takes time. Whether it's counseling, moving out of the house you're in, cutting off a toxic relationship, going to work so you can become independent, getting plugged into a healthy church, forgiving someone or whatever you need for healing, find the support you need. There comes a time in everyone's life when you're knocked down. You will either stay down wallowing in self pity or you will pick yourself up, dust yourself off and take your next step.

Perhaps Rocky said it best when his son was playing a victim instead of taking personal responsibility for his own future in *Rocky Balboa*:

> *"And when things got hard, you started looking for something to blame, like a big shadow. Let me tell you something you already know. The world ain't all sunshine and rainbows. It's a very mean and nasty place, and I don't care how tough you are, it will beat you to your knees and keep you there permanently if you let it. You, me or nobody is gonna hit as hard as life. But it ain't about how hard you hit. It's about how hard you can get hit and keep moving forward. How much you can take and keep moving forward. That's how winning is done! ...you gotta be willing to take the hits, and not pointing fingers saying you ain't where you want to be because of him, or her, or anybody! Cowards do that, and that ain't you! You're better than that!"[1]*

Summary

I have not walked in your shoes, and I have not felt your pain. If you've had severe trauma in your life, I feel for you. I really do. I have seen it in my students, and it breaks my heart. However, I have also learned that many people will use their issues as a crutch or an excuse that keeps them from reaching their full potential. Healing is hard work; overcoming crap that this world throws at us is hard work. When we look around at successful people, it's easy to play the comparison game. Then, we are tempted to tell ourselves and our friends the lie that he or she is successful because they never had serious issues. This lie, though, will hold you back. The truth is that everyone has skeletons in their closet. Everyone has baggage. You don't know the ugliness that others have had to overcome to get where they are. Will it make you bitter or better? That's your choice. Choose wisely.

"No one tells parents that it's actually possible to pay cash for college."

—Anthony ONeal, author Debt Free Degree[1]

Chapter 21
Everybody gets student loans.

[Even if you don't plan on going to college or already have a degree, you will know people in the future who will go to college, so I encourage you still to read this chapter so you are prepared to have a productive conversation with them on the topic.]

There are so many lies about college that it's hard to know where to get started, but this is the lie that I think might be the most damaging. Believing that everyone gets student loans and you have to also is destructive on two different levels.

First, it gives you the mindset that student debt is normal and inescapable, so you are more likely to let your guard down and end up not actively finding ways to avoid or keep student loans as low as possible. This reactive, as opposed to proactive, position you assume is likely to cost you literally *thousands of dollars*. You will be more likely to miss out on scholarships, work study programs, and other financial opportunities at school. You'll likely spend more flippantly throughout college with a mindset of I'll just pay it back later. Because of these missed opportunities and excess spending, the extra loans and compounding interest on those loans can balloon to a number of dollars far beyond what you imagine.

Secondly, once you buy into this lie, you are strapping yourself with a ginormously heavy burden at the exact time you are trying to launch yourself independently into the real world. When you need freedom and margin, you have shackled yourself with debt, interest and an unnecessary large monthly payment. With the false assumption that student loans are unavoidable, you almost certainly will get student loans or have markedly higher loans; therefore, when (or worse, *if*) you graduate, you are going to be starting the rest of your life with a mountain of debt. Sure, you should be earning a decent salary to help pay it off, but the reality is that paying off student loans takes much longer and is much more burdensome than most people expect.

It has gotten so bad that it's actually referred to as the student loan *crisis* today.

I feel like I'm a smart guy, but I had no practical idea how financially oppressive student loans could be. I graduated with a Master of Arts in Teaching in 2004, and after paying about $300 monthly, receiving $5,000 loan forgiveness and then paying a lump sum of around $5,000 more at the finish line, I finally broke free of my student loan debt chains in 2021. It was like a weight was lifted off my shoulders! I ran some rough numbers just for funsies because I'm a nerd. On approximately $50,000 of student loans, I repaid approximately $65,000, and that is after the $5,000 that was forgiven!

Oh, and the cost of college has roughly doubled since I went to school.

People act like this is normal…well, it kind of has become normal, but it should not be! In general when people talk with older teens about their future, there is a tendency to be more hopeful and less doom-and-gloom which is understandable. Downplaying the legitimate

150

concerns of repaying student loans, however, paints a false picture to young people whose brains and cognitive decision making processes are still being formed. They are innocently lulled into this false narrative that you can borrow money for college, then get a good job and quickly pay it back in a couple of years.

Statistically, that *almost never* happens.

According to the Education Data Initiative, "The average student borrower takes 20 years to pay off their student loan debt."[2] Instead of a period at the end of that sentence, there should be an exclamation point or two.

Twenty years! That's the average which means about half of people who take out student loans take *longer* than twenty years. You know who plans to take two decades or so to pay off their student loans? Almost no one. So we can reasonably conclude that most people who take out student loans will carry their "student loan baby" much longer than anticipated.

And that's only the monetary side of the equation.

"The negative effects of student loan debt aren't just financial," Dave Ramsey said. "We found that 53% of those who took out student loans regretted it. And 43% of those who took out student loans regret going to college altogether."[3]

I know a woman who recently earned her Ph.D., and in typical modern American fashion, she has loads of student loan debt to go with her degree. There's only one problem. She doesn't really want to work. Her husband is making a decent income, and they have a few kids. She would prefer to stay home, but it's almost impossible for her not to work full time…because her monthly student loan payment is so massive.

When you have student loans, you greatly limit your options. The loans can affect where you live, what jobs you can take (or not take), when you can comfortably have kids, your spouse's job options, your peace of mind, when you can buy a house, the quality of your relationships–especially with your spouse, what car you can afford, how much you can save and invest, how much leisure time you have, your future nest egg and a host of other things.

In case I haven't been clear, student loans are almost always a bad idea. If you still don't believe me, google "student loan horror stories," and click on two or three of the millions of results.

For those of you who are thinking about scamming the system by taking out a bunch of loans and then getting them forgiven, well, not so fast. In his book Debt Free Degree, Anthony ONeal notes, "Less than one percent of people who have applied for student loan forgiveness actually received it."1 Those odds are kind of like playing the lottery.

Now that I have dealt with why taking out student loans is such a poor decision, let me offer you some hope.

You can go to college without student loans.

Yes, really!

For starters, an article from Forbes gives these statistics on college students:

"55% of students from public four-year institutions had student loans," and

"57% of students from private nonprofit four-year institutions took on education debt."[4]

Yes, this means that the majority of college students have student loans, but it's actually a relatively small majority. Another way to look at this is that nearly half of college students do NOT have student loans! Others–over 40% of students–have already discovered that NOT taking student loans is possible and are currently living that reality. You should join *that* club!

Doubters will suggest that it's just rich people paying for their kids, but that's also a lie. That is only a fraction of those without student loans.

So how do normal people pay for college without student loans?

I'm glad you asked.

First of all, they study. Making good grades and learning the academics and how to think critically are probably the prerequisites for getting college paid for. However, even if you're not a straight A student, college can be affordable.

People who want to graduate from college without debt think outside the box. In the box, the only option is student loans. Outside the box, there are many options.

Here's a bright idea: get a job! Before you dismiss that, many college students have jobs to help cover their extra expenses like food, transportation, clothes, social activities with friends, etc. Also, working part time actually correlates to a higher GPA than students who don't work at all (or students who work full time). Apparently, the time constraints cause them to prioritize and utilize their limited time better.

The other benefit of getting a job is that more and more employers are paying for college. Major fast food chains, pizza joints, coffee shops and department stores have funds for college and so do many smaller businesses. If they do not, it doesn't hurt to ask. Many small business owners might have never entertained the idea, but perhaps they will reconsider when their hardest working employee sits down with them to discuss the possibility of helping them get their college degree.

Next, make scholarship hunting an artwork. One of the biggest regrets of my life was when my dad came from work with a stack of scholarship applications and, after thumbing through them for five minutes, I dismissed them completely. That lazy, dismissive and unappreciative attitude probably cost me tens of thousands of dollars. I'm kicking myself right now just thinking about it. Don't be me. Learn from my mistake, so you can live with more freedom than I had for those 17 years of student loan debt.

Go to your school counselor. Look up local scholarships from your area. Google scholarships for your field of study and anything unique to you. Ask the financial aid departments at the colleges you are wanting to attend which scholarships you need to apply for. Start submitting the scholarships that require essays. These often have fewer applicants. You may be rejected for 90% of them, but that means if you apply for 50, then you'll receive five! Think about it like this: you'll receive 0% of the scholarships you don't apply for. Ten to twenty hours of work on this is likely to reward you thousands of dollars.

Many different organizations have funds that can cut the cost of college. This might be an honor society or organization that has scholarships that high school students can apply for. It might be a service organization that you apply to through your college and then have to volunteer for so many hours to get a deduction on your tuition.

I know a girl who just received a similar scholarship of $5,000 every year by serving 75 hours per semester on campus. When you do the math, she is basically getting paid well over $30/hour.

154

Many schools have very lucrative compensation for on campus jobs. Being a resident assistant (R.A.), working campus security, editing for a school newspaper or social media and working in the college daycare facility might pay well, have discounts on your school bill or both. Just run the numbers. A $20/hour job might seem great, but if you can do something else to get free housing which could save $6,000-8,000 per year, that might be better.

Also, think dual credit in high school, community college, state schools and online programs.

Dual credit courses are often free or super cheap. A three hour college class costs around a couple grand, while often the fee for the same credit hours as a dual credit class in high school might be 100 bucks. That's a 95% savings on that class! Another big financial advantage to having high school dual credit is that students have the potential and flexibility to graduate early if they are intentional and plan their classes accordingly. For students who find academics and studying more challenging, they have the flexibility to take smaller class loads during different semesters if needed and still graduate on time.

Everyone is aware that community college is cheap or often free in many states by keeping a modest GPA and meeting other minor requirements. What people seem to forget is that when someone completes two years of college at a community college or junior college, they often have an Associates Degree. This is a big advantage because students have earned a marketable degree, have a couple more years of wisdom and experience to know what field of study they want to pursue, have no student loan debt clouding their decisions and have more options moving forward.

If you're lucky, you might have the option to take dual enrollment classes through a local college to earn an associates degree by the time you graduate high school!

There are three traditional public high schools in Bradley County, TN. There is also a local community college. The college has partnered with all three high schools through the Tennessee Valley Early College program (TVEC). At the beginning of every May in recent years, about two dozen or so high school students graduate with their associates degree from the college before walking across their high school stage a couple weeks later to receive their high school diploma! If you know any promising middle school students, you might want to see if this is available in your area.

State schools are another good option. Not only do state schools usually have the most affordable costs, but they also often have the most straightforward scholarship process for basic merit and in-state scholarships. Some people have a negative perception of state schools, but these perceptions are largely unfounded. Going to private or exotic colleges might seem better but that's often not true. For starters, there have been a number of studies about how comparable most degrees and salaries are regardless of school (Ivy league schools withstanding). Additionally, transportation is usually cheaper, easier and quicker to and from home to college. Finally, the cost difference is often so great that most times the state school makes better sense. Many people have borrowed thousands and thousands of dollars to attend private or out of state schools only to regret it later.

Another option to stay out of debt is looking into online programs. These options are more for non-traditional or self-motivated students, but depending on your circumstances, it might be a fit.

Let's address one little push back here before wrapping up this chapter. Many teens will say that they just want to go off and have the college experience without having to work and be stressed about money so they'll think about it later. In a parallel universe, that sounds lovely. But in the real world, can you see the irony of how at the exact time they are becoming a legal adult, they are avoiding adult conversations and decisions that will literally impact the rest of their lives? Going to college might be the first adult decision they make. If so, how to pay for it, should be the second. Also, do they want to get married? Do they want to have kids? Do they want to have options after they graduate? How will $100,000 of student loans affect these plans and dreams?

If you are a parent, you may consider funding an ESA or 529 plan if you strongly feel your children should go to college. You don't have to be rich to do this. You can have 50 bucks, 100 bucks or whatever you choose transferred automatically each month. The interest earned is typically tax free. The sooner you start, the more it will grow. Talk to someone where you bank and go online to learn more.

When my grandparents passed, they left a modest amount of money to each great grandchild. I put most of this into an ESA for each of my children and chose a mutual fund. I didn't do anything else except check the monthly statement in the mail. I never deposited another dollar. By the time my first child is heading to college, that account has grown to more than double. (Returns are not predictable, so talk with your financial advisor.) It's definitely not going to cover all of my kids' college, but everything helps.

After reading this, hopefully you believe or are on your way to believing the truth that graduating from college debt free is possible.

Summary

Student loans should be the exception not the norm. Student loans are not necessary or mandatory. Don't believe the lie that everyone gets student loans, because the reality is that nearly half of college students don't. If you want more thorough information on going to college without debt, I recommend Anthony O'Neal's book *Debt Free Degree*. If you have a few minutes and are interested in a blunt and humorous take on the harsh reality of student loans check out "Dave Ramsey's Epic Rant About Student Loans" on YouTube. There is also an engaging documentary called *Borrowed Future* that you can find on various streaming services.[5] The truth is that not everyone gets student loans and you don't have to either. If you want to go to college, do it the right way so that it's a blessing and not a burden. Explore your options. Make a plan. Go get your degree and start your future debt free!

"Don't ever take sides with anyone against the family again. Ever."

— Michael Corleone in The Godfather II

Chapter 22
No Matter What, Always Have Your Family's Back.

Many people consider The Godfather movies (at least the first two) to be among the best movies of all time. Led by Marlon Brando, Al Pacino, and Robert Duvall, an all star cast portrays the family dynamics of love, loyalty, rivalry, jealousy, compassion, kindness, resentment and grace perfectly in one of the most intriguing settings, the Italian Mafia in New York.

Its wide viewership now spanning over 50 years has also made it one of the most quotable movies.

When Michael turns his head, looks his brother Fredo in the eye and coldly warns him: "Don't ever take sides with anyone against the family again," chills run down your spine.

It was such a powerful line, that untold thousands of people have repeated it. It has been quoted, paraphrased and retold countless times in countless situations to countless people. Think about it. Those words were spoken in the context of a mafia family, yet you will hear the same sentiment with close to the same level of gravity in nearly every culture and setting in America. You will hear it in rural, suburban and inner city America. It doesn't matter what race or class, the deep loyalty of having your family's back no matter what is a shared common value.

The idea of having your family's back was not a new revelation in *The Godfather* series, but the intensity, fervor and blind loyalty with which you are expected to have your family's back, never taking another side was likely new for many.

Loyalty is a good thing.

Family is a good thing.

Loyalty to family is a good thing.

Blind, zealous loyalty to family without boundaries…not such a good thing. Even Michael Corleone who so intensely lectured Fredo about not taking sides "against the family" has Fredo–his own brother–murdered later.

Michael had a boundary, and if it was crossed, or crossed enough times, he no longer had your back.

Now, I'm definitely not telling you to resort to violence against your family. Please don't do that. But I am telling you not to give your family a free pass to do whatever they want and still keep them in your inner circle.

In theory, and often in reality, your family should be your inner circle. This circle typically starts with your biological family or the family you grew up with. As you get older, it often changes. Usually parents and siblings are in this circle, especially at the beginning; however, cousins, aunts and uncles, grandparents or grandchildren and close friends may move into this circle.

Outside this circle, there are friends. These are the people you like to be around and usually both of you make an effort to continue the relationship. These are often your neighbors, close colleagues, members of similar interest groups and/or people you went to school with for an extended period of time.

The outermost circle comprises your acquaintances. These are the people with whom you have somewhat regular contact for a reason, but if that reason stopped, then so would the relationship. In my life, these people are some of my colleagues, some people I play pickleball or basketball with, some people at my church and various people in the small community I live in that I've gotten to know over the years and see around town.

"Blood makes you related, loyalty makes you family," is a popular meme and often shared and reposted lately.

That is a good start, but I prefer another viral quote, "One of the biggest lies ever told is that blood makes you family. Blood makes you related. Loyalty, love, and trust make you family."

With that in mind, who is your family? Not your biological family, but who is your real family? Often many biological family members are your real family, but sometimes not all biological family members deserve to remain part of your real family.

College and professional athletes often talk about their team being their family. Fraternities and sororities often feel like family. Some people refer to their "church family" or "school family." Many armed forces and service members refer to those they serve with as family. Even gang members will refer to one another as family.

There are a number of other examples but my point is that for various reasons, family changes over time. The people you would list as family when you are 13 is probably different from who you would list when you are 23 or 43.

Sometimes, who your family is changes naturally, or it happens effortlessly. People move away. People move close. You get a new job or a new hobby. You get married. You have children. You get divorced. You might have an experience that brings you closer to someone.

I have had two different weddings 15 years apart. My brother, my cousin and a third man were groomsmen in both. A number of other groomsmen were different. Shortly after college, I was a groomsman in two different weddings of which I've hardly seen the groom since. Inner circles change. Your family changes.

There are also times that who your family is or is not results from more intentional effort.

Growing up, I had roughly seven uncles and seven aunts (divorce, death and remarriage changed the numbers). Often we'd get together for family reunions or other events up and down the state of Florida. Sometimes, one aunt in particular wouldn't show up. I didn't know why then, but later in life, I learned one of my uncles basically banned her from his property. Apparently, there was a legal issue between her and a family member, and a third family member made the conscious decision not to allow her on his property again. I don't know all the details or who's to blame for what, but it was clear that someone made a very conscious decision on who would no longer be in his inner circle.

Decisions like this are rarely easy, but you need to have the courage to make the hard decision of removing people from your circle of trust, from your "family" when their actions require it.

I had to make a similar decision when a close family member of mine started clearly taking sides in a sensitive family situation. It was painful. I love this person. This family member is a good person; however, trust was broken and things were done that caused another family member great hurt, and from my perspective, unfair and unnecessary hurt. I didn't write a mean letter. I had a couple conversations, and it became clear that this person was being stubborn, refusing to listen to reason and was on a hill that she would die on. So I just let it go. I wasn't hateful. I still send a Christmas card, but otherwise, I no longer actively work on that relationship. I'm not going to have someone's back who I know is clearly wrong and causing others I love pain.

Now, I want to shift a little bit. What about your boys? Your guys? Your girls? Your homies? Your teammates? Your entourage?

You have to have their back, right?

I would say, in most things, yes.

In all things? Heck no!

This is when wisdom is needed. This is when defining decisions are made. This is when reason and logic are your friends. Raw emotion is the killer of sound reason. Both emotion and reason are good, but they help balance each other.

When you get caught in a situation where a member of your family does something you disagree with, how will you respond? Obviously, there are different levels. Nobody is perfect, so everyone will make mistakes. I have family who check me when I do something boneheaded or vice versa, but there are also lines that we know can't be crossed or we risk losing one another.

I mentioned this story earlier, but it's worth repeating here.

When I was going through my divorce, I was emotional. I could see the train wreck coming, so I called one of my guys. We talked. Then, I went out and wrecked the train anyway. I felt bad, so I came clean with him the next day.

His response was quick. It was sharp. He let me know that he'd be there for me when I needed, but if I didn't listen and wouldn't take his advice, then I shouldn't waste his time. While I was a little hurt by his bluntness, I also respected him.

My friend, my man, my buddy, my brother drew a line in the sand that he was not going to participate in my foolishness. I also realized that I was at risk of losing having him in my inner circle. His words were hard to hear, but you know what? I needed to hear them. It helped give me clarity and make better choices moving forward.

He loved me enough to tell me the truth. He loved me enough NOT to always have my back. He loved me enough to say that he would not participate in my self destruction, and I appreciate him for it.

Think about it. Thousands of people have been convicted for being an accessory or accomplice to a crime because someone else was doing something criminal and their friends or family didn't have the courage to say, "No, I'm not going to participate in this."

This often leads to not only the one who committed the crime being found guilty, but also the accessory or accomplice also being convicted. Why do that to yourself? More importantly, why participate in someone else's self-destruction?

If you truly are someone's family, often you will have their back, but there are sometimes, that the best way to have their back is not having their back.

Perhaps no story illustrates this better than the kid who received only 10 years of probation for killing four people while under the influence with the "affluenza" defense.

The news reported that Ethan Couch was raised in a wealthy family who never set boundaries or disciplined him. He pretty much

164

did whatever he wanted. As a teen, he stole beer, got drunk and had an accident killing four people and seriously wounding others. It was reported that the prosecution asked for 20 years. The judge gave him 10 years...not behind bars, but probation. He violated probation a short time later, and his mom had his back so much that she helped him escape to Mexico to avoid getting caught. (Both were later extradited back to the States.)

At times, "having your family's back no matter what," only enables that person to be more and more destructive. Boundaries and consequences are healthy. When you protect someone you love from any and all consequences by having their back, you actually allow greater harm to come on them. Sometimes, the best way to have their back, is not to have their back and let them face the ramifications. If they are in that position, they obviously aren't listening to your advice; therefore, natural consequences might be the only voice they'll heed.

Summary

Having your family's back is a good thing most of the time. People need help, love, support and encouragement among other things. However, don't believe the lie that you *always* have to have your family's back. In fact, there are a number of times that having a family member's back will be the worst thing for them. Loving your family well encompasses many things like cheering them on, being there for them, helping them get up when they fall, showing them grace when they make a mistake and also setting a boundary when they go too far. At a certain point, don't participate in a family member's bad decisions. You have to decide where that line is. When you set this

165

boundary, often they will respect you for it, and you just might be saving them from severe repercussions down the road.

"Sometimes people have sex because they don't feel good enough. Because they lack self-worth."

– Justin Bieber

Chapter 23
Everybody's doing it.

[The specific reference of this lie is that virtually every young single person is having sex before or outside of marriage.]

The most believable lies are those that are mixed with truth. This is also what makes these lies some of the most dangerous. This is true for many of the lies we've discussed, but it is especially true for the lie that everybody's having sex.

While it is true that many or rather most young people are sexually active before marriage, it is definitely a lie that *everyone* is. There are a number of young people who value virginity before marriage and are intentionally choosing not to have sex. Many regular people have successfully kept their "v-card" until marriage. Even a surprising number of celebrities have chosen to forgo sex outside marriage, but we'll delve into that a little deeper later in this chapter.

When I was a teenager, I can't tell you how many times I heard, "Everybody's doing it," or, "Everybody's having sex. I mean, everyone that can find someone."

Most of these conversations were with peers, and it didn't matter which peer group was having the conversation, there were a number of people who all voiced this same sentiment. On the surface, this seemed accurate at first, especially in larger group settings. *Hardly anyone objected*, but later I learned this was mostly out of fear of becoming a target. What teenager wants to be the center of attention when it comes to this stance? What teen wants to be stared at by wide disbelieving eyeballs and then bombarded by pointed, invading questions insulting her or him for being a prude? Typical teens would run like a cow from a cookout at that kind of vulnerability.

However, the tone often changed when the size of the group got smaller and the peer group was more of a close knit group of friends who could be a little more honest and open, having confidence that one's words would be received with a higher level of respect and understanding. Apparently, a surprising number of my acquaintances and friends were still virgins into their late teens and even twenties. Some even had this crazy-sounding Utopian idea of not having sex until their wedding night.

In my early-mid teens, I remember hearing a speaker named Ron Luce talking about staying a virgin until marriage. This was one of the first times that I gave intentional thought to it. He was religious, but he didn't come at it from that perspective. Luce instead argued that sex was awesome and that the best, ultimate sex could only be experienced between a husband and wife in a committed marriage. He talked about more than just the physical side of sex, but also the emotional, psychological and spiritual aspects of sex, something most young people seem oblivious of. He talked about how most things are better when you wait and experience them at the right time. He also talked about the value of sex, the value of each person and the value of the gift of virginity. I just remember coming to the realization that there was a whole lot more to sex than what my friends talked about and what was on TV.

From a historical perspective, many ancient societies valued virginity. There are some exceptions, but a thorough review reveals that for many societies, virginity was respected, desired and valued in various ways. Specifically, the Greeks, Romans, ancient Chinese, Hebrews and Zulus (the great sub-Saharan African tribe) all highly valued waiting until marriage to have sex. Many other Middle Eastern, European, Asian, Native American and African cultures shared similar values.

One caveat is that in some of these cultures, exceptions were more readily made for men losing their virginity before marriage than women. Even with this double standard being taken into account, it is clear that many, perhaps most, cultures historically valued sexual fidelity even if only for one gender. *[For the purpose of this chapter, sexual fidelity will be defined as having sex only with your spouse.]*

Americans sometimes have an arrogant tendency to think we know better than everyone else. When it comes to sexual freedom and expression, a couple generations ago the majority of Americans held a similar perspective to these other cultures, still respecting and striving for sexual fidelity. Now, however, the pendulum has swung to the opposite side and most people expect their future spouse will have had multiple previous sexual partners.

This rapid change begs a number of questions. *What changes in society caused this shift in expectations? Why has something that was so valued for so long by so many now become so much less valuable? Was this the right or wrong change? What can we learn from this?* And so on.

These questions open the door to so much information and interpretations that people have written lengthy books on the subject, so

169

it is impossible to address all aspects of this significant change in the way our culture perceives sexual fidelity. However, there are a few brief logical points I want to make on the subject.

First, I'd like you to consider the possibility that current sexual practices around much of the world are less the result of proactive logical thought but more of the result of gratifying lustful desires fed by the increasing access to pornography over the recent few decades. Just think about it for a minute. Try to unbias yourself from any quick reactive defensive objections and just follow the logic.

Not long ago, to access porn, one used to have to walk into a shady gas station or the back room of a video store, pick up the magazine or video, and go to the cashier. You actually had to look someone else in the eye (or hold your head in shame) to access adult content. A handful of teens would find a stash, possibly at a neighbor's house, and access it that way, but this was risky, unreliable and had concrete time and place constraints.

Today, however, most high school students, many middle school students, and a growing number of elementary students have potentially unlimited access to porn almost anywhere and anytime in their pockets.

Let that marinate for a minute. Our society has evolved, or rather devolved, into a society that allows *children* to access porn at their fingertips.

Sure, there are parental controls, but how many kids know the workarounds and tech better than their parents? How many eight year olds are accessing porn on a regular basis in our society? Why are we not protecting them better? Is it the parent's responsibility or the government's responsibility? If it's the parents, how many will fail to restrict...

Ok, back from that rabbit trail.

Adult magazines such as Playboy magazines in the 1950's were much more mild than in the 1980's and 1990's. Adult content in video was much less widespread and accessible a few decades ago. Most of that same video adult content was also less explicit. Mainstream movies had little sexual content until the 1980's. On regular TV in the 1990's, there was zero nudity. Paying for movie channels could open the door for more adult content, but sex and nudity was still often limited until late night hours on these channels. And the internet? Well, I, like most of my friends at the time, graduated high school without ever being on the internet.

In fact, a not uncommon question among junior and senior high school guys was, "Have you ever seen a porno?"

Some guys didn't even know what that was.

Compare that with today.

As a middle school teacher I've had different trainings and heard all kinds of statistics on how early children are exposed to porn. Depending on the source, the average age of first exposure is typically between 8 and 12 years old. That's an average which means many kids' first experience is even younger. If you're skeptical, ask any middle school educator or upper elementary teacher if they ever have issues with students trying to (or succeeding in) accessing porn on school devices.

There are two noticeable trends over the recent few generations. One is that the production, distribution, access to and consumption of pornography has greatly increased. The other is that sexual activity and/or promiscuity among unmarried people has increased. (Some research suggests this latter trend may very recently be decreasing among men and their partners, but I would suggest this is likely because these men are now meeting these desires through a screen at home instead of with a physical partner.)

Is there a correlation between the two trends? I feel that not only are they related, but the first has directly led to the second. It's simple logic really. Men are visually stimulated. Regular media has much more sexual nature now. Access to graphic illicit media is much easier; therefore, it is consumed at a much greater rate.

What is the result?

This has changed men's sexual expectations for how women should behave, what women should do, and how early they should do it. Women are also watching this same media that portrays sex as much more casual, normal and even empowering. Additionally, the pool of *men* who happen to value sexual fidelity has decreased, which is an issue for *women* who also value sexual fidelity. I don't intend to sound cold, but this creates a simple supply and demand problem. Some ladies are pressured to either lower their standards or stay single indefinitely. This can be a big issue or crossroads for these ladies, but it is significantly greater for women who are wanting children because their time is limited.

It doesn't take a degree in rocket science to conclude that current sexual practices around much of the world are less the result of proactive conscious decision making but more so the result of gratifying lustful desires and the growing sexual expectations. These sensual desires and expectations have been created by our media's widespread increase in normalizing and celebrating sexual relations and the growing distribution of and access to porn over recent decades.

The next point I need to make is simple and old school; however, that does not make it any less true. Sexual fidelity generally leads to stronger marriages which in turn has been observed as the best way to raise children. Most cultures from the six livable continents practiced a traditional husband, wife and children family unit. This practice has been largely successful for millenia. Sure, exceptions exist and one's bias might quickly search for said exceptions, but the reality is that sexual fidelity creates stronger bonds, trust, peace and stability in the marital relationship which is felt throughout the home. Numerous studies and articles over the years refer to this as "the marriage advantage."[1,2,3]

[Note: you might come across articles that appear to contradict the marriage advantage because recently there has been a push to disprove these findings. You'll notice the articles are laden with bias and a lack of solid data.]

I would also like to remind you that waiting often leads to improving something and making it better. Aged wine and cheese are much preferred to wine and cheese that have not aged enough. Kids that visit amusement parks before they are tall, and possibly brave enough to ride all the rides they'd like to often don't get the full experience. My son was nearly heartbroken when he wasn't able to ride the Wild Vortex, a trap door water slide, that he was dying to go on at Wilderness at the Smokies. People who get large car payments instead of waiting to pay cash often find themselves upside down on their loan and frustrated with their decision. Similarly, people who buy *too much* house often have buyer's remorse and end up "house poor." Some people take vacations on credit cards, but stress about how they are going to pay it off the entire vacation or the next few months after they return.

I'm not trying to be a killjoy or the fun police. In fact, if you look at it from my perspective, I'm helping you improve the quality of all these things. Go to an amusement park when you can afford it and your kids can enjoy it. Get a car that will be a blessing and not a burden. Maybe you have to wait a couple years...so what? Put your car payment into a savings account for three years and then buy that car outright. Your vacation should be a time to relax and splurge on some luxuries, not to stress. Buy a smaller house or save for two or three more years to have a bigger down payment to buy the house you want. When you wait on your wants and desires until the right time, they are much more satisfying, and you will fully appreciate them much more.

So it is with sex.

Delayed gratification is a concept that psychologists have used to describe people saying, "No," to an immediate pleasure *now* so that they will receive something better *later*. Using delayed gratification also has a strong correlation to being more successful in many areas of life.[4]

Waiting to have sex until you're married has many benefits. For starters, you will definitely have much more self-control. Your spouse is likely to trust you more since you haven't been sleeping around and have demonstrated that you can control yourself. There won't be people in your life that are awkward to be around for you and your spouse because you used to be sexually active with them. There is also an emotional bonding aspect of sex for many. This bonding with others won't have a detrimental impact on your marriage. Many people have a sense of shame, hurt, guilt, regret, low self-worth, embarrassment, trauma or other negative feelings about past sexual experiences, and you won't have to worry about carrying these into your marriage either.

Finally, one of the best reasons to wait until you're married to have sex is because sex is valuable, you are valuable and so is your spouse.

Sex is awesome! It really is. It shouldn't be shared commonly like a walk in the park with your buddy. Sex is special.

How special? That depends on you and how much you value it.

You also are valuable. Unfortunately, many young people today have been hurt and lied to. Many young people don't know how valuable they really are. Maybe you've made some mistakes. Maybe you were abused. Maybe you don't think you're pretty. Those things don't define you. Every person has worth. Start believing that. Start living that. Even if you've had sex before, you can make a decision that from now on, you'll only have sex with your spouse.

That's what Mariah Carey and Nick Cannon did. Neither of them were virgins, but they made a joint decision to wait until they were married.

The first celebrity I heard, or read, of that mentioned waiting until marriage was "Iron Man" and three time NBA Finals champion L.A. Laker A.C. Green. But there have been many others: Tina Fey, Russell Wilson, Jordan Sparks and Tim Tebow to name a few. Even Justin Bieber said he waited. Of course, we can't really fact check them! The point is that there are many more people who are waiting to have sex than you probably expected.

Your spouse is also valuable. Think about her or him. Ideally you will spend roughly 50 years of your life with one person that is often referred to as your soulmate. That's kinda heavy. How important is that person to you? How valuable is your spouse? Is he or she valuable enough to wait for a few years without having sex? I guess the answer to that question is up to you.

Summary

I know waiting to have sex until you're married is hard–extremely hard! But isn't pretty much everything in life that is extremely hard ultimately worth it? Do Olympic athletes complain that the thousands upon thousands of hours they invested were too hard? Do doctors and lawyers despise the years of study? Do the everyday people who train for a year or two or three wearing out many pairs of shoes to run a marathon regret it? No!

Some people will even go as far as telling you that waiting until marriage is impossible. But it's not.

I know this personally. I got divorced in 2017. My former spouse and I weren't healthy and continued our physical relationship for a short period of time after the divorce. Eventually, I came to the realization of just how unhealthy my behavior was and how destructive it would be to *my* future and, more importantly, to my future spouse. At some point, I made a commitment not to have sex again until I was married. For a man in his mid thirties after having had a regular sex life for 13 years, that's a pretty big adjustment! It's a complete paradigm shift. I knew waiting would be so challenging that when my current spouse and I started talking seriously, I told her I didn't even want to kiss a woman until I was married–I knew if I started down that road, it would be a slippery slope. That said, I want you to know we waited until we were married, and it was well worth it! (Full disclosure: we got married about six months after we started talking, and the brief courtship was definitely helpful.)

Don't believe the lies that everyone is doing it, so you have to too.

"There came a moment when I realized I was doing all the talking and no listening on this subject."

–Rob Schenk, former activist (before switching sides)

Chapter 24
Lies about abortion.

[Hours of research on both sides' strongest arguments, time at pregnancy centers, conversations with medical professionals and friends/family on both sides of the issue and watching numerous videos of the pros and cons of abortion went into writing this chapter. Some of the data shared is not cited because it is readily available from many sources (both pro-choice and pro-life sources).]

This is absolutely the most difficult chapter for me to write. I know full well I'm running the risk of deeply offending anyone and everyone, from those I've never met to my wife, to my mom and dad, to my children. What is more is the gravity of the subject and how it could significantly impact some of the most vulnerable people in society.

So why write it?

That answer is simple: I care enough about you–and your entire generation–to tell you the truth. With social media and the internet, I believe never have so many lies been told so repeatedly and so forcefully to a generation. I feel convicted to speak truth into your life, even hard truths…especially hard truths.

I have one request. Please do not read this chapter until you have read the previous chapters. It is not possible for you to receive this chapter adequately and fully appreciate it the way it is intended if you read it in a vacuum. Just like a good friend or family member of yours can talk to you in a way that strangers cannot, so it is with this chapter. Reading this without first reading the other chapters, getting a chance to learn my heart and motives will likely leave you defensive, angry and close-minded.

If being defensive and close-minded is the path one chooses, I cannot keep you from it, but I believe most people want more for themselves than that. I think most people are tired of one-sided, gas-lighting rants and genuinely desire intelligent, open-minded conversation in which they can both listen and share respectfully.

That said, if you have not read the previous chapters, please stop now and go back.

If you have read them, please proceed with an open mind.

I want to begin by acknowledging three things:

1. Abortion is an extremely divisive topic.
2. I have my own opinion on the topic and stand on one side.
3. I will not share that opinion in this book as that is not the goal of this chapter or the book.

So what is the objective of this chapter?

The objective is for your generation to recognize two brutal lies, learn how to handle these lies with more maturity and grace, start to truly consider the pros and cons of both sides, and learn how to live together despite differing opinions.

Lie #1 is that every person who is pro-life is a chauvinistic woman oppressor who wants to control women by taking away their rights.

Lie #2 is that every person who is pro-choice is a heartless baby murderer who refuses to give an unborn person the same rights they enjoy.

Are there some heartless baby killers and chauvinistic woman oppressors in our society?

Sure.

Are there 100 million or more of each?

I don't think so.

So how did the abortion debate end up classifying the entire country as one extreme or the other?

Well, the simple answer is politics.

Politicians and champions of causes find it easier and more expedient to demonize their opposition than to have patient, respectful, productive dialogue.

As consumers we're all guilty of contributing to this. Our society is driven by click-bait because what are we more likely to read: an article about two authors debating the data on pros and cons of reproductive rights or an article highlighting one woman's near-death experience from either her delivery or her abortion?

While a handful of people might choose the former, the vast majority of us are more intrigued by what happened to the woman who nearly died. This is human nature. However, human nature and a human's first instinct are not always best.

For instance, it is human nature to run immediately from a burning house, but if your best friend, child or someone else is asleep in the next room and you run without waking them up, it might not have been the best decision. It could have been a very deadly decision.

It's very easy to get passionate when talking about killing an unborn child or discussing white, conservative lawmakers wanting to control women. In fact, it is natural for these accusations to stir your emotions. Emotions are good and helpful. So is logic. As people mature they begin to balance these…well, at least reasonable people.

If you watch certain guys on Fox News or gals on The View, you might not see much evidence of a logical side, but in general as people grow up, they learn how to better balance their emotions with logic and self-control.

And I'm asking you to do this. Think maturely. Think critically. Be intentional about thinking through the rest of this chapter with as much open mindedness and logic you can muster.

Here we go.

The abortion debate has deteriorated into less of a thoughtful debate and more of a gaslighting fight by intentionally, drastically misrepresenting the opposite side.

One group says they are pro-choice. That's a positive spin, so another group calls them "baby killers."

The other group claims to be pro-life. That's equally positive, so now the opposite group calls them "chauvinistic woman oppressors."

Just stop and let that marinate.

Are those really the only two options? Is everyone either a woman oppressor or a heartless person who could care less about babies?

Well, let me let you in on a secret.

Those aren't the only two options.

It is possible to be pro-life and also pro-women's rights. (Some of you won't agree with that statement.)

It's also possible to be pro-choice and love babies. (Others of you won't agree with this statement.)

Regardless of whether or not you agree with me, I'm going to tell you the truth.

Here's the truth. There are women who have had abortions who have also had babies and love those babies.

Here's another truth. There are women, and men, with rock hard pro-life convictions who fully support women and women's freedoms.

Yes, both of those statements are true. Don't believe the lie that you can't be pro-choice and also love a baby. Don't believe the other lie that you can't be pro-life and also fully support women.

Don't be fooled into thinking it's that easy. Don't bite on that lie. The truth is often difficult.

Truth is also exclusive, meaning two opposite statements can't both be true. People will use this to try to manipulate their argument to exclude what they don't agree with. They will try to make two statements seem opposite that are not opposites in a sly attempt to discredit the opposite side.

For instance, someone might say that the grass is green and since trees are not grass, they can't be green. But these are not opposites; therefore, this logic is flawed and wrong. In reality both grass can be green and so can trees be green.

Truth can be challenging. Truth stretches us. Right now, it's about to get painful. Pain is good. It helps your muscles grow.

But this pain is different. It's going to help some closed minds grow. (Insert mind blown emoji here.)

If you are pro-choice, I challenge you to think of why your side always refers to the unborn as a "fetus," "tissue," "mass of cells" or similar term?

Conversely, if you're pro-life, why does your side always use the term, "baby"?

These terms are very intentional. One side seeks to dehumanize what is inside the womb so it can be thought of as a routine procedure like getting a cavity filled. The other side wants to humanize what is in the womb so it can be thought of as an intentional act of ending a life.

As with many of life's important questions, the truth often lies somewhere in between. There's nuance. There are extenuating circumstances. Not every situation is the same.

It's like what that frustrating teacher would always say when you asked those burning questions in middle school, "It depends."

"Depends on what?" you ask.

I'm glad you asked. Let's dive further into the messiness.

For starters, when does life begin?

You really can't answer whether abortion is right or wrong, until you answer this question. Those on one extreme say that life begins at birth. Those on the other extreme say life begins at sex.

Spoiler alert: they're both wrong.

If you need a crash course on "the birds and the bees," you're in luck: I'm a teacher.

When a man and a woman have sex, a man will orgasm. Millions of sperm will be released into the woman's vagina and will start their seek-and-fertilize mission of the woman's egg in the fallopian tube. Whether or not this is successful is largely influenced by the timing of her menstrual cycle. If the timing is right, the sperm can fertilize the egg and a fetus is conceived.

Depending on the source you choose, conception takes from a minimum of hours to a maximum of around three weeks. At or shortly after conception, boom, there's new DNA, in the fetus. Within a month, it has its own blood and heartbeat. Not long afterwards, the fetus gains many of its features and movements. It continues to grow and develop, and the general consensus is that viability is by the 24th week.

"Viability" means that the fetus can now survive outside the womb. This timing is noteworthy because typical pregnancies last 40 weeks (4 months after viability). (Babies surviving from the age of viability outside the womb have a much higher percentage of success where modern medicine is available.)

So, when does life begin?

I don't have the exact answer, but I'm confident that both, "at sex," and, "at birth," are wrong.

Conception often takes days, so it's difficult for anyone to claim that life begins at sex. Additionally, some might argue that it still takes time for the body's systems to develop and even have a heartbeat. On the other hand, since a baby is viable at 24 weeks and there are plenty of living examples walking among us, it's hard to see how it can be argued that the baby is not alive at or near this point.

Now that we got that out of the way, let's go even deeper.

What about cases of rape and incest?

What about these cases after the point of viability has been reached?

What about cases in which a woman just casually has unprotected sex regularly?

Should the father have any voice in the decision making process?

Is there ever a point at which an abortion should be halted?

What about cases in which the life of the mother is at stake?

What about the morning after pill? Or what about in the 39th week?

At what point should the baby's life be considered? Or should it ever be considered?

What if the mother is on drugs, living in poverty and already has kids?

What if the mother doesn't want to give up the child for adoption?

What if the child will likely have a major disability?

What if the mother wants a child later in life (but not now) and used contraception but still got pregnant?

Many of these questions are not easy to answer. If you have easy answers to all of these, you are in real danger of hypocrisy-either side!

Many pro-choice people want the mother to have the right to choose all the way up to birth. Well, if that is the case, how can you demand freedom of choice for one individual (the grown woman) and deny it to another individual (an extremely viable 38 week baby with his or her own DNA that is different from the mother's)?

Many pro-life people want all babies to be born; however, many of these same people also want less government services provided to help many women in need. If one truly is pro-life, that person would be fighting for the success of the mother and baby long after the baby is born, would he not?

Many pro-lifers spend the majority of their energy fighting for the unborn to be born but neglect assisting the lives that are already being lived. This is especially concerning when considering the number of babies born to single mothers in poverty. Some of these babies do grow up to overcome their circumstances; however, it is more likely that many of these babies will grow up in poverty, in an abusive environment, without an adequate education, to a life of addiction, to long term depression or mental illness, have a greater risk of being incarcerated or a combination of these negative lifestyles.

What about fathers? Does the term "pro-choice" only apply to mothers? Is it not hypocritical to demand freedom of choice for women and deny the same for men? What about child support? Is it fair to *require* child support and expect a parental presence from someone who had no *choice* in the decision making process?

Some will argue that it's a woman's body; therefore, she gets to choose. While not perfect, this sounds like a strong argument…until you get to the point of viability, then this argument falls to the same shades of hypocrisy if one is not going to assign the "my body, my choice" logic to the viable baby.

Let me ask you a couple direct questions.

If you are really *pro-life*, what are you doing to help already born people currently struggling in poverty, with addictions, who are homeless, who are being raised by single parents, who are in the foster care system, who are at greater risk of being incarcerated, who have PTSD, etc. Is it not hypocritical to stand on a "pro-life" platform and fail to help these *lives*? Or to weigh the options of abortion when the *life* of the mother is at increased risk?

If you are really pro-choice, what about the *choice* of the fetus or baby? At any point during pregnancy, is the choice of the fetus considered? Is it not hypocritical to stand on the "pro-choice" platform and never consider the choice of the baby, particularly after viability? Is it not just as hypocritical not to consider the *choice* of the father?

In a day and age in which everyone screams for transparency, both sides of abortion seem to be willingly, almost deceptively, untransparent when it comes to certain issues involving abortion.

In our quest for truth, let's shine more light on this, in spite of how much discomfort it might bring.

First of all, you can find videos of virtually *everything*, no matter how good or how sick, on the internet. But if you search for an ultrasound of a third trimester abortion, you get nothing. Why? Because it's gruesome and it opens Pandora's box when it comes to women's reproductive rights when pitted against what others would refer to as murder.

Some might argue this example is unfair, while others would argue *not* mentioning this example would be unfair. Like many of one's biases, it depends on which side of the fence you sit on and who you're defending.

If we had scaled this example back and asked about watching an abortion in the first or second trimester, the temperature of the room, and also your blood, would not have jumped as high, but there would still be significant questions and concerns.

On the flip side, how many people have actually sat with a thirteen year old child who has been raped by a family member and

188

listened to the terror and trauma she has been through? Then, are you going to tell her she must carry this fetus to term, she must give birth to the baby, and she has the option of giving it up for adoption?

Many people in the pro-life camp want to talk about the PTSD and other serious long term mental health issues some women who have had abortions face yet neglect to address mental health and the long term life burden of many women who gave birth to a child they might not want or are not ready to have and lived with the impact for the remainder of their lives? And vice versa for the pro-choice camp. To address one side of women's mental health without addressing the other is not only unfair and short-sighted, but continues to keep our country divided.

What would happen if as a country we quit helping only the hurting women that supported our causes, but started helping all women, especially those who are politically different than us?

Summary

On Christmas Eve of 1914, British troops and their allies were entrenched in their battle lines when they heard German troops singing *Silent Night* in German. Recognizing the tune, the British joined the chorus but in English. While other factors were involved this led to the spontaneous Christmas truce of 1914 in which soldiers from both sides met in "No Man's Land" between the trenches for camaraderie, sharing family photos and football (soccer). Afterwards, the soldiers were less than zealous to kill the men they had bonded with the day before, and the policy of *No Fraternizing with the Enemy* was born.

I encourage you to do the same as these soldiers did over a century ago. People with opposing viewpoints are not your enemy. They are people. You don't have to agree with them. Try just listening.

Like Steven Covey suggests, "Seek first to understand, then to be understood."[1]

I challenge you in the pro-choice (or women's reproductive rights) camp to research Gianna Jessen, Abby Johnson and Bernard Nathanson and learn their stories.

I challenged you in the pro-life camp to research George Tiller, Laurie Bertram Roberts and Rob Schenk and learn their stories.

And as a note, don't read a biased representation against their stories, but learn their stories from their own words.

For you overachievers who want additional homework, text or email one friend who you know has an opposing view than you and politely ask them to share their rationale on their side when they have a chance. Once you receive their message, just reply with a brief appreciation but don't share your side (unless they genuinely ask).

And don't forget the truth. There are many pro-life people who also are very much pro-women, and there are many pro-choice people who also love babies. Quit demonizing those who don't think exactly like you on this subject. You can still be pro-life or pro-choice: *that* is your choice.

"Boys don't cry."

– A father with a heart of stone and whose family doesn't care if he's around.

"Weak people avoid conversations that are challenging. Strong people welcome them."

– Unknown

Chapter 25
Counseling is for the weak-minded.

Thankfully, this is one of the lies that is currently getting weaker instead of stronger. Most of the mainstream media has already come to the truth that counseling is often positive and that people who participate in counseling are not weak. However, this lie still has a powerful hold on certain groups, particularly young men, athletes, men of color, and people across different parts of the South.

Growing up playing sports competitively and still playing pickup basketball and recreational softball into my forties, I've been around athletes my entire life. It has been a common view among many of these types that counseling is only for "softies" and not for real men and women. Yes, it's common for both genders.

Only recently has seeking professional help for one's mental or emotional well-being become more acceptable. And while understanding and accepting that "others" may need counseling, there remains a large percent of athletes who still feel it is a sign of weakness, at least for themselves personally. Living in Tennessee for 25 years now, I've also noticed this same sentiment from many men.

And while there is a growing cultural acceptance of counseling, there is also a second lie that stems from the first lie. As people start to accept counseling as more normal, many people have limited its benefits to *others*. It's almost like they are saying, "Counseling is okay…for you."

This is the reality for many, and not just for men. A lot of women also feel this way, particularly in marriages and relationships. Everyone wants *everyone else* to go to counseling because we all so easily see others' issues, yet we are often blind to our own.

Perhaps the best illustration of one's natural blindness to one's own faults is the ironic story of world-renowned British journalist and author Malcolm Muggeridge while living in India last century. During a morning swim in the Ganges River one day, Muggeridge noticed the silhouette of a naked woman bathing in the river not far away. Few people were about at this early hour meaning he could act on his fantasies without much risk. As a white man in India, the woman might even welcome his advances. Driven by erotic desires, he stealthily swam over to the lady. Reaching her, he stood up out of the water, and to his horror, he was face to face with a leper. Years of leprosy had disfigured the woman's entire body. Her face was a terrible sight as her nostrils and lips were deteriorated or missing. Even her skin seemed to be decomposing all over her body.

Shocked at this ugly creature standing before him, the thought of how hideous she was flashed through Muggeridge's mind. *Hideous creature*. As he swam off, another thought occurred to him.

She was not the hideous creature.

He was the hideous creature.

He was about to engage in the lusts of his flesh without concern for anyone else. He was about to commit adultery at the least, break his vows to his wife, and risk devastating his children. His heart was more hideous than her appearance.

It's so easy to see the flaws in others.

I have news for you. No one is perfect. We all have issues.

What are your issues?

Stop, and chew on it for a minute.

Seriously, stop.

Ask yourself: "What areas in my life do I need to address?"

Verbally, name at least two or three things you need to improve about yourself. Say them out loud, or write them down. You can write them in the margins in this book. Get out your phone and list them on your notes.

If you haven't yet come up with at least a couple areas of your life that need some work, guess what, you are holding yourself back. You are limiting yourself and your future success. We all have room for improvement.

How are you going to improve? What areas do you need to improve? Do you have trauma from an abusive past, being abandoned, the death of a loved one, betrayal or other PTSD? Do you have anger issues, anxiety or depression? Do you have an addiction like alcohol, gambling, gaming, porn, social media or drugs? Do you feel inadequate because of something that happened in your childhood? Does your significant other complain that you can't empathize or are absent emotionally?

Again, no one is perfect. What area in your life needs addressing the most? How are you going to address it? Is it something that counseling can help? Are you open to counseling?

The good news is that not every person needs counseling. However, I think every person can benefit from good, healthy counseling.

Is all counseling great? No.

Are there "quacks" out there? Sure, but there are also many good counselors.

Not everyone requires counseling, but a heck of a lot more people do than actually go. I can't tell you how many people I know who wound up getting divorced but never went to more than a one or two sessions of counseling because they "didn't have time." Apparently, they had the endless hours and days of meeting with lawyers, preparing for and going to court, dividing up their household belongings, finding a place to live, moving out and restarting their life, but they didn't have an hour once or twice a month to go to counseling for a year.

Good counseling is not a waste of time, it's actually the opposite. Quality counseling will significantly speed up your healing process which makes you a better person and gives you much more time later.

If you're still not convinced of at least being open to the possibility of counseling, consider this man's journey leading up to counseling.

He had the body of a Greek god. As a first team All-American, he led his college football team to the national championship. He was the NFL Offensive Player of the Year his rookie season, a three time

Pro Bowler and retired top 20 on the all time NFL rushing list. Year after year, the 185 pound back ran toward 11 men, some twice his size, who trained their entire lives to catch him, grab him, push him, tackle him, drag him, pound him to the ground as hard as they could, yet this was not as intimidating to him as a one-on-one counseling session.

You may have figured out that I'm referring to Warrick Dun who I wrote about previously. A teammate called out Warrick one day after practice for his lack of joy in life, and Warrick realized he needed help. I want to share some quotes from the fifteenth chapter of his book *Running for My Life* because I feel Dunn's words cut to the heart of the issue better than mine.[1]

"There is a broader cultural taboo about going to therapy."

"The fact of the matter is that counselors, psychologists, therapists, shrinks–that whole realm is really looked down on in the African American community."

"It's viewed as a sign of weakness."

"And here I was supposed to open my guts, talk about my mom's murder, and spill my emotions."

"I insisted that I wanted everything to be kept quiet about my identity."

"The clinic made arrangements for me to park and enter behind the building."

[Referring to the first session] "I couldn't look Dr. Clance in the eye."

"It took several more sessions before I was able to start looking up at her."

"By talking things through...I finally realized...I needed to relieve myself of that burden."

"I started relaxing more. I started having more fun. I just think I became a better person."[1]

The progression from fear, hesitation and anxiety to healing, peace and joy is easy to see in these few short quotes. Your story has different details than his and mine, but if there are major issues in your life, counseling can help you address them adequately so you can have a similar ending–a happier, peaceful ending.

Just in case you're curious, here are some other celebrities who are upfront about how counseling has helped them: Michael Phelps, Harry Styles, Michelle Obama, Bruce Springsteen, Selena Gomez, Brad Pitt, Katy Perry, Michael B. Jordan, Prince Harry, Jay-Z, Jennifer Lopez, Jennifer Anniston, Jennifer Garner, Robert Downy, Jr. and many others.

The benefits of counseling are plenty. For some people, just getting things off their chest relieves a burden. For others, processing things out loud helps them regain a sense of order and peace. For some, the counseling process makes challenges or pain more manageable. For some, it helps understand others better. For some, it helps understand oneself better. For many, it's a combination of these.

The last thing I want to mention is the benefits of group work. This isn't the same thing as counseling, but there are similarities. I had a friend who lost his wife, and he told me how helpful attending a grief group (for those who had lost loved ones) was for him.

Similarly, I attended a Divorce Care group for about a year. Divorce is terrible. It can be downright painful, but going on the journey was so much more manageable with others who had walked the same path. I didn't want anyone telling me how to feel or what to do who didn't *know* the agony I was in.

On another note, the struggles of a blended family are real. I love each member of my family, but having people in my house who have been stretched across three homes with three different routines and cultures, with various parents and step-parents, two separate parenting plans, and schedules of up to 10 children (six under my roof) demanding which kids and which parents are where and when and who is responsible for what expenses can be a nightmare. If you're not in a similar situation, frankly I don't want advice from you, but I'm more ready to listen to someone who is familiar with and faces similar challenges.

Group work and small groups can be so beneficial because the relationship of others who are in similar situations is invaluable. That's why Alcoholics Anonymous and three dozen or so other groups patterned after it have been so effective. Finding a group of people that have been where you've been is often one of the best ways to move forward, know you're not alone, get practical advice from what they have experienced, and heal.

Counseling is not for the weak-minded. In fact, the opposite is true. Counseling is for those who have the *strength* to face their problems, the *humility* to own their shortcomings, and the *courage* to start the healing process.

<u>Summary</u>

Don't believe the lie that counseling is for the weak. Don't believe its sister lie that only other people need counseling. You may or may not need counseling, but don't shut the door to it. Be open. Where are you in life? What kind of person are you? Do you respect yourself?

Do others respect you? On a scale of 1-10, how is your relationship with the three closest people to you? While not everyone needs counseling, the truth is that most people will benefit from good, sound counseling. The truth is that people who go to counseling have courage. They are strong enough to do some real reflection. Looking at yourself in the mirror is hard work. Don't wait for a staring-a-leper-in-the-face moment. Are you strong enough to go to counseling if you need it? If you've gotten this far, I know you are.

"One big difference between a man and a woman is that if a woman says, 'Smell this,' it usually smells nice."

-Unknown

Chapter 26
There's not much difference between boys and girls.

Now that's funny!

If you can't laugh at that quote above, you need to put this book down and pick up one entitled, *How to Find a Sense of Humor*...or at least look up, "Jeff Foxworthy smells," on Youtube and watch a couple videos.

But seriously, boys and girls are different, and the differences are significant.

First of all, I never nursed any of my children. True story. Not much explanation is needed. My wife nursed though. Sure I fed them bottles, but that's not quite the same.

Next, my wife never impregnated another person, and she can't. Neither can any other woman. Again, I don't see the need for an explanation...

Moving on, my wife likes me to have a beard. I do not reciprocate the same sentiment towards her. To my knowledge (and deep appreciation), she never has sported a beard and never will.

In a similar vein, or follicle if you will, my chest resembles a shag carpet. Again, my wife and I differ here. Fortunately, we both appreciate the features the other possesses.

And my back...well, for your sake, let's set a boundary ~~hair~~ here and move on.

Another physical difference between the two of us, and everyone agrees, is that she's miles more beautiful than I am.

The last physical difference I care to mention is that I can lift, carry, move, push, pull much more than she can. Yes, I weigh about 50% or so more than her, but this muscular difference is consistent for genders across large enough groups of people and confirmed by countless scientific studies.

In fact, I remember a thought-provoking case study in my college sociology class 25 years ago about the qualifications of firemen. For whatever department it was, one of the physical qualifications to start training was carrying 125 pounds (or there about, I've forgotten the exact amount) over your shoulder a certain distance. This was to simulate carrying someone out of a burning building. Historically, there had only been men at this fire department, but women began to apply. While a handful of women were able to pass all the other physical tests, none of the female applicants were able to pass this test. This test was modified, only for females, to allow them to drag a certain amount of pounds a certain distance. The community was greatly torn between whether or not this compromise was beneficial and acceptable.

I'm not sure what the final outcome was in this case, but I do remember much of the discussion and even conflicting opinions in my own mind. Of course, women should be allowed to be firefighters if they can pass the same tests. However, since there is such a small percentage of women that can pass all the same tests, this effectively eliminates over 95% of all women. That leads to a miniscule percentage of women who both can pass the physical test and who also actually *want* to be firefighters. What about the women who can pass all the other tests except this one? Surely, it's fine to modify this test just for them. But what if *my* dad is in a burning house on the floor, do I want a different standard for the firefighter who has seconds to pull him out?

I'll be the first to admit that I don't have a perfect answer to this case study. I feel at least slightly uneasy either way it's settled.

But the physical standard for firemen isn't the point. The point is that men and women are different. Even having the case study indicates there is a substantial difference. It's the same struggle for the military, FBI, some police academies and other physically demanding fields.

Did you notice I interchanged the word, *firemen* and *firefighters* in the previous two paragraphs? I intentionally did that just to get you thinking. I'm so old that when I was growing up, I don't even know if *firefighter* was a word back then. We always used *fireman*, but that is definitely an inaccurate term now to describe many *firefighters* (more widely accepted term now).

The simple truth is that men and women are physically different. The difference is so great that when doing physical testing, different standards exist for different genders.

This is also true for competitive sports. While genders are often combined at younger ages, as kids mature, more competitive leagues are divided by gender. Logical people tend to agree that at higher levels it's not in the best interest to have an all boys basketball team play an all girls team; however, one lady used this to her advantage.

Former University of Tennessee Volunteer head coach Pat Summitt has earned Olympic gold, eight NCAA National Championships, multiple Hall of Fame inductions, 32 SEC championships and other awards too numerous to list. For nearly four decades, her teams were among the best in the country. There are a number of factors for this, but one of the main reasons is that she had her players practice against guys. Why? Guys were quicker, stronger and bigger making her players tougher and better all around. Since then, nearly every major women's college basketball program has followed suit.

The difference becomes even more serious when considering higher contact and violent sports like wrestling, football, hockey, rugby, lacrosse, etc.

Yes, there are exceptions to every rule, including this one. I'm aware there are some gray areas, and that people sometimes want to push their agenda over logic and try to point toward rare cases in which there might be an exception.

I'm not making blanket statements that cover 100% of humanity. Please, let's be reasonable. When people start reaching for a one-in-a-thousand example to prove their point, I think they've already missed the point and they're beyond reason.

That said, I recently heard Bill Maher share a quote by Massachusetts Congressman Seth Moulton that I really had to chew on. I'm hesitant to share anything political because a political agenda is not the goal of this book. The *truth* is what this book seeks, and I think Moulton's honest, vulnerable words challenge people to search for truth over personal bias and agendas so much that I feel it would be disingenuous of me not to include it.

"I have two little girls, I don't want them getting run over on a playing field by a male or formerly male athlete," Moulton admitted. "But as a Democrat, I'm supposed to be afraid to say that."[2]

Wow, what honesty! When's the last time you heard such honest truth from any politician, Democrat or Republican? That statement might be career suicide, but the man chose truth over agenda. You have to respect that.

The glaring physical differences between males and females are undeniable, but what about the intangible differences? Well, they are just as great but are a bit more difficult to recognize. And since we're seeking truth, we're gonna do the hard work to find it.

Let's begin by reminding ourselves there are exceptions. Yes, there are some manly girls and girly men, but we're not debating in the margins here. We're looking at the vast majority of humankind.

There are a plethora of books, studies and literature highlighting a number of differences between men and women. John Gray's *Men are from Mars, Women Are from Venus* or Deborah Tannen's *Genderlect* research and theory are two examples that had been standard reading in higher academics for a while.[2,3] Recently, however, there has been pushback on the differences between men and women and the mounds of supporting research. Newer studies challenging years of data and conventional wisdom have popped up, but *it's hard to tell how legit the studies are versus how agenda-driven they are*.

Let's examine some of the differences from an open-minded perspective. Men are more daring (or dumb) from a young age on. Think about boys riding bikes and creating their own ramps. In my childhood group of friends, if you had recorded how many times the boys and girls needed a band-aid, I'd guess it was probably 3-1, maybe 4-1, boys to girls. My buddies and I were always being bandaged up. The girls did on occasion but not so much.

If you doubt this difference, just ask car insurance companies what the data says. That is why car insurance premiums cost more for teen boys than teen girls.

Also, the girls always talked and dreamed about getting married and what their wedding day would look like. The boys and I thought about it once in a blue moon but never sat there day-dreaming about it. In fact, none of us ever really cared (or even thought) much about the decorations. Having had two weddings now, I can tell you the bride had an entirely different perspective on the decorations than I did.

There is a *nature vs. nurture* argument, but it doesn't hold much water in many of these examples. In fact, now that I mention it, women are far better nurturers.

Just think about it, when was the last time you walked into a daycare and all the employees were male? In fact, if I were going to drop my baby off at daycare and all the employees were male, I'd walk out with my baby, and so would most of America. There is a difference in the trust we will place in *who* is taking care of our babies.

Men have less patience for young children's foolishness. I did my student teaching in 1st grade for two weeks. It was awful. My wife is a first grade teacher. She is the best first grade teacher I've seen, and I don't think there is a man on earth who could do a better job in her classroom. Literally, she is that amazing in that classroom! Conversely, she has zero desire to teach middle or high school.

Statistics also reflect this. Roughly 75% of all teachers are women. However, this figure grows to about 90% at the elementary level and drops to about 60% at the high school level. Elementary schools actually love having male teachers, but the pool of male applicants is just so tiny.

Speaking of education, in my personal experience with around 2,000 students and having taught alongside 20 different teammates over the last 20 years, I have noticed kids respond markedly differently to men and women.

Now, there is a *nurture* issue that comes into play here. Kids might be raised by a single parent or two same gender parents. A kid might be abused by a parent. A kid might be neglected by a parent. Whatever the reason, there are some kids who respond differently based solely on the teacher's gender because of how they were treated by a parental figure of that gender (whether positively or negatively) growing up.

There is also a strong nature component to it. I have connected with many students that my female counterparts have not and vice versa. There are certain students who will either act out or behave much more in different classes based solely on the gender of the teacher. Beyond that, there is an overall different set of expectations by students from day one when entering my or my male teammate's classroom compared to our female counterparts.

Sadly, statistics reveal a somewhat similar theme for inmates, depending on *who* was in the home when they were growing up. The large majority of people who are incarcerated have a common theme: they come from a fatherless home. The statistics vary from source to source, but nolongerfatherless.org reflects, "85% of youths in prison come from fatherless homes."[1]

The first time I fully realized this was when a local non-profit organization was trying to help at-risk youth in our community. I sat there dumbfounded seeing statistic after statistic of the negative impact on children who grow up without fathers. The stats extended beyond incarceration also to depression, dropping out of school, drug use, prone to violence, living in poverty, etc.[1,2,3]

The same statistics weren't the same if the single parent was a man. Having a father in the home provides a sense of rules, structure and boundaries that are sometimes absent without a father.

Conversely, children raised in motherless homes tend to have higher rates of anxiety, greater trust issues, are likely to struggle more relationally and are more stoic.[4]

There are a number of other common-sense differences that might not have as many data points but are experienced.

As my kids were growing up, disciplining my children was very different. My daughters took much less effort in this area. In fact, I could have made them melt to tears just by looking at them harshly. My son, on the other hand, also had a soft spot but required more frequent discipline and at higher levels.

Currently in my house, my wife and I have different expectations from each other and also for our children. The boys and I usually take out the trash, do the yard work, put up the Christmas lights outside the house, move the heavy furniture and items, etc. The ladies tend to be more involved in decorating, baking and some cleaning. We all help cook and clean the dishes, but my wife probably does the most here.

Yes, these things are nurtured, but they reinforce what is from nature, and I conscientiously do certain things. For instance, I open doors for my wife. She is fully capable of opening a door, but this act of kindness makes her feel respected, so it is my privilege to do that for her. The trash can be gross, so I take it out or ask our boys to do it. She knows how to check the oil in her car, but I do it for her. She can carry heavy boxes, but it is much more of a strain for her, so the boys and I do it so she doesn't have to. She can grill a steak, but I do it. She can take the car to get the tires changed and sit in a greasy waiting room or talk to the mechanic about why it's making that sound, but I do it.

Why do I choose to do these things? Am I contributing to my wife becoming a prissy lady who can't do anything for herself? Absolutely not! She is capable of doing all of these things, but if I am available, I willingly do these more masculine things so she doesn't have to get sweaty and dirty. She, like most wives, appreciates her husband doing these types of things effectively so she doesn't have to worry about them, can relax and focus her energy and attention on other things.

On the flip side, I appreciate the banana bread and cookies my wife bakes. I appreciate our house being decorated nicely...the thought of decorating for the next season never even occurs to me. When I get home from work and the kitchen is spotless, I love it. I'm thankful for her knowing where all the kids are supposed to be, at what time and how they are getting there. I appreciate her regularly making sure the whites are bleached.

Does she ever take out the trash, check the oil or carry a heavy box or vice versa? Of course! There are times, we each help the other; however, she doesn't want a feminine husband. That would not help her feel safe or secure. Neither do I want a masculine wife. I love my kind, soft, tender, joyful bride, and I appreciate her that way.

Our differences don't create an inequality. Our differences are complementary. They help us effectively meet all life's demands and run our home while showing each other love and respect. It's not perfect, but it's efficient, cozy and beautiful.

Summary

I didn't even get into issues like chromosomes, left brain vs. right brain, sexual drive, amount of time on video games, menstrual cycles, watching sports vs. romcoms, rates of maturity, going to the restroom in groups, etc. The truth might not be politically correct, but then again, being politically correct is not my purpose. Speaking the truth is my purpose. Boys and girls are different, and men and women are different. Those differences are huge! These differences don't make either gender superior or inferior. They simply exist. We do ourselves, our society and the next generation a disservice and harm when we don't have the courage to recognize and communicate the truth that boys and girls are indeed different, and it's okay that they're different.

"Even God himself couldn't sink this ship!"

- Titanic Captain Edward John Smith

Chapter 27
There is no God.

The most reasonable philosophers are aware that it is impossible to prove or disprove the existence of God. Think about it for a minute. If there is a supernatural being–by definition superseding natural laws–who creates a universe and its life forms which are limited by the natural laws He created, can they definitively prove the existence of their Creator?

No. They are finite. God is not.

Well, if that's the case, is this chapter meaningless?

Absolutely not! Although we as humans are limited by natural laws, we still possess (or have been blessed with) great powers of observation, reasoning, personal experience, philosophy and scientific experimentation.

When one weighs and logically considers the possibility of God in an unbiased manner, he will be left with a huge mountain of reason and evidence that points *toward* God, instead of *away from* a higher power.

For starters, what happens when God is deliberately removed from society as atheistic cosmologist Lawrence Krass would like?

"If we can plant the seeds of doubt in our children, religion will go away in a generation," Krass suggested, "And that's what I think we have an obligation to do."[1]

This exact scenario actually unfolded roughly a century before Krass when in 1882, the famous German philosopher Friedrich Nietzsche so boldly proclaimed, "God is dead. God remains dead. And we have killed him."

Nietzsche's philosophy quickly spread across the modern world at the time being taught in many of higher education's elite universities. The impact of Nietzsche on Adolph Hitler is well documented and, ultimately, how Hitler fashioned Nazi Germany for its violent takeover of Europe, establish brutal concentration camps and carry out the Holocaust.

Furthermore, this violence was not only a logical outcome of removing the belief in God from so many in a generation, it was actually predicted by Nietzsche himself who rightly guessed that the 20th century would become the bloodiest century ever. By some estimates, more people were murdered in the 20th century than the previous 19 centuries combined. The amount of bloodshed was monumental: WWI, WWII, the Korean War, Hitler's Holocaust, Joseph Stalin's regime, Mao Zedong's reign, the Rawandan genocide among other African conflicts, Middle East wars, the Vietnam War, other Communist regimes like the Khmer Rouge, etc.

Simply put: when God is removed, chaos follows.

Some will argue that even with God, many nations and powers have contributed to great violence referencing the Holy Wars, slavery, etc. On the surface, this appears to be a solid argument, but its weak foundation becomes apparent when you dig a little deeper.

The truth is that the violence stemming from a philosophical worldview of life without God is a rational progression. If there is no God, what gives life value? Who sets the rules? Where do morals come from? One values his family or his country. Your people are in the way of his people's success, progress and happiness. He wants to eliminate the competition. This is not the only logical progression, but it is a natural progression and, unfortunately, history has recorded this violent pattern over and over and over again.

Conversely, violence and murder that have been perpetrated by people who claimed to believe in God, particularly Jehovah, the God of the Bible, is logically contrary to a *Biblical* worldview, particularly the teachings of Jesus. When the average person was illiterate and Bibles were scarce, spreading false teachings in the name of God was much easier. Now that nearly everyone has access to a Bible, it's much more difficult to twist a vague verse here and there to deceive the masses.

Just consider these words of Jesus:

"You have heard that it was said, 'Eye for eye, and tooth for tooth.' But I tell you, do not resist an evil person. If anyone slaps you on the right cheek, turn to them the other cheek also. And if anyone wants to sue you and take your shirt, hand over your coat as well."[2]

It's a logical inconsistency to treat others violently and also claim to be a Christian. People can claim to be anything they want, but that doesn't make it true.

A funny story about Muhammed Ali has been retold more than a few times. When Ali was on a flight and turbulence caused the "fasten seat belt" light to come on, a stewardess asked Ali to buckle up.

"Superman don't need no seatbelt," Ali said confidently.

211

To which the stewardess replied, "Superman don't need no airplane either."

Ouch!

The man who regularly referred to himself as "The Greatest" was humbled by a lowly flight attendant.

Don't miss the point. It is true that people have done bad things in the name of God or Jesus, but that doesn't mean that they were Christians or actually God followers. In fact, their actions were contrary to the Word of God.

While we're having a philosophical discussion, consider a few more philosophical points.

First, a life without God is a life without purpose. Some might argue otherwise, but try as they may, those arguments are left wanting. If there is no God, how did we get here? The Big Bang and evolution over billions of years? If so, then humans are no more than the result of the right chance mixture of elements and matter arising from cosmic gook. What would give us Homo sapiens purpose? Nothing.

Even the Nobel Prize winning outspoken atheist Bertrand Russell was in full agreement with this conclusion saying, "Unless you assume a God, the question of life's purpose is meaningless."

Secondly, life without God, conveniently allows people to do whatever they want with no accountability (outside the rule of law *if* they are caught). They get to make their own rules and values.

Modern philosopher and former New York University professor Thomas Nagel is candidly open about how his atheism and desires intersect.

In *The Last Word*, Nagel wrote "I want atheism to be true and am made uneasy by the fact that some of the most intelligent and well-informed people I know are religious believers. It isn't just that I don't believe in God and, naturally, hope that I'm right in my belief. It's that I hope there is no God! I don't want there to be a God; I don't want the universe to be like that."[3]

It's unclear if this is an outright confession by Nagel, but you have to respect the honesty in his words. Embracing atheism has a major conflict of interest: if there is no God, then *you* get to be god.

How so? Well, who decides what's right and wrong? If there is no God, then there are no morals. You might object here, but do a quick Google search. For thousands of years (at least since the Greeks), people have argued over morals, ethics, laws, etc. and outside of God, there is zero consensus. Without God, people don't have to follow *another's* rules, they can make up their *own* rules and live by them. They can *play God* to themselves. They don't have to submit to anyone else's rules. It's extremely convenient.

Another point to consider is the most common argument against God. It can be phrased as either a question or a statement.

If there is a God, why does He allow so much pain and suffering in this world? Or *with all the suffering in this world, there can't be a God.*

I will be the first to admit that even I find this logic somewhat troubling-especially when I think of innocent children being abused. Emotionally, it hurts.

Philosophically, however, dissecting this argument leads to a very direct and logical path most folks won't see coming.

What exactly is being said when people suggest that a good God would not allow so much pain?

Well, in essence, the point is that since innocent people (particularly children) suffer, there can't be a good God because He would not allow it. Basically, there ought to be less suffering in the world. Most people would agree.

But *where* did that "ought" come from?

Who is to say what "ought" or "ought not" be?

When people are in consensus that things "ought" to be this way or that way, they are referencing a universal moral law (ethical code). When we agree that innocent children ought not be abused and subject to intense suffering, we have already acknowledged (whether consciously or subconsciously) a universal moral law.

If a moral law exists, it has to come from a *who* or *what*.

To simplify, if one argues there can't be a God with all the pain and suffering in the world, this argument acknowledges a standard (moral law) of the way things ought to be. Once this moral law is recognized, one has to consider where it came from. Since morals are apart from the natural world, the most logical source is a moral law giver. This moral law giver is more commonly referred to as God.

So when people base an argument for no God assuming a moral law, they are actually embarking on a logical path that points toward His existence.

Let's move to the realm of science.

You might find it interesting that Isaac Newton said, "In the absence of any other proof, the thumb alone would convince me of God's existence."

This quote is nowhere close to definitive proof of God, but it is some food for thought. Just think about how many different thumb prints exist? What about its DNA, which no two people share? Even identical twins who were once thought to share the exact same DNA, are now being found to have differences. The waterproof skin, the millions of cells, the bones, the veins, the arteries, the capillaries, the blood, the cuticle, the thumbnail and the tendons stretching down to the muscles in the hand all work together for your opposable thumb. This single appendage allows you to shuck corn, weave a basket, play the piano, swing a bat, zip up, button up, pop the top on a can of soda and turn a page in this book.

This stub protruding from your hand is pretty lucky for an evolutionary mutation that occurred when a bone accidentally sprouted the wrong way out of a hand millions of years ago...

Or the thumb was created with intentionality and purpose.

Which is more likely?

Speaking of whether or not the thumb evolved or was designed, one should contemplate how we got here–scientifically.

There are only two reasonable views: the big bang leading to evolution and the lesser accepted idea that a supernatural being created the universe.

To say the cosmos came from God admittedly takes faith in the supernatural.

But doesn't suggesting life came from a big bang take just as much faith? Or perhaps even more faith?

Think about it. We're being told that random gases and elements whose beginning remains *unexplained* mixed at the right temperature in the right proportions in the exact right distances from any celestial bodies or black holes (as to not float away or be brought to rapidly together) to start the space-time-matter dimensions of our universe.

On top of that, you are then expected to believe that from this matter, life spontaneously burst into existence. Wow! That takes another big leap of faith!

[Some argue that the life forming wasn't *spontaneous*, but reason leads one to recognize that life had to have a beginning at a particular moment in time. Therefore, how else could one describe the moment before this life began until the immediate moment after it began except *spontaneous*?]

Even if you buy both of those...uh *miracles* (for lack of a better word), isn't it most likely that this life form would have almost certainly died right away? So to believe that this life (perhaps a single-celled organism or smaller) was able to reproduce takes another drastic leap of faith. Then to believe that this life form reproduced and evolved over the years by eventually sprouting limbs and feathers and gills and sight and tusks and web-slingers and talons and esophaguses and toe nails and tentacles and scales and echolocation sonars and pouches and nanocrystals that allow a chameleon to change colors and escas that allows an anglerfish to hold a lighted lure in the darkness, etc. takes a whole other degree of faith.

Many people will stop here and argue that there is a mountain of scientific evidence backing this last statement like fossils records, rock layers, observation of species changing like Darwin's finches, carbon-14 dating, etc.; however, most of this "scientific evidence" ultimately tells a different story if examined through an unbiased lens. (See "Bonus Chapter for Nerds" if you are interested.)

The fact of the matter is that if one could truly study the science from scratch with zero preconceived ideas about the age of the earth or how the universe came to be, they would be left with two thoughts:

1. While there is an abundance of evidence for microevolution (changes within a species or to a new species that is closely related to the first species), there is an extremely minimal amount of hard evidence that macroevolution (large changes like from one kind to another) has indeed occurred.

2. There is just as much (if not, more) evidence for a young earth, as in thousands of years as opposed to millions or billions of years. And if the earth is not millions of years old, then the theory of evolution is impossible.

These two thoughts lead one to no other alternative except to at least consider divine intervention. (Again, see "Bonus Chapter for Nerds" if you take issue with the validity of either of these conclusions.)

Another interesting idea is the numerous hospitals that have chapels. Have you ever wondered *why* so many hospitals have chapels? Most other major buildings don't have a universal chapel. Might it be because when many people are forced to face their natural finite self in a mirror (or the death of a loved one), they finally get serious about connecting with a Higher Power? Lives that were lived fully without any concern of God often have a dynamic paradigm shift in their final days and hours as they lay down all preconceived notions, begin to truly consider His existence and explore a relationship with Him.

Then there are the stories: personal stories, historical stories, recent stories, recorded and documented stories that all share a common theme of supernatural intervention.

In early 1775, an avalanche in the Italian Alps buried a small town. After a week, rescuers and family members quit their search efforts and waited for the spring thaw. Weeks later a man had a vivid dream that his wife was still alive. With newfound determination, he managed to locate and uncover his house, but she was not there. Then he dug out the barn and found not only her, but his daughter also and a third woman. They had been buried alive for 37 days.

In 1943, a bomber crashed in the Pacific Ocean 850 miles from Oahu. Former Olympian Louis Zampirini and 2 other men survived the crash. Although not a man of faith, Zampirini began bargaining with God. Zampirini told God about how he would live if God saved him from the ordeal. After 47 days adrift on an inflatable raft with holes, shark attacks, storms, being strafed by Japanese planes, he was rescued from the sea...only to go on to be physically and psychologically tortured at four different POW camps until his release in 1945. After battling PTSD and alcoholism upon his return to the U.S., Zampirini found God, lived another 50 years serving others, especially at-risk youth. He even returned to Japan to *forgive* his tormentors.

On March 1, 1950, at 7:27 p.m., a church exploded in Beatrice, Nebraska. Due to the sternness of the choir director, the fifteen members were often early and rarely late. Not a single person died. For the first time ever, the entire choir, including the director, was more than seven minutes late on the same day. The odds of this happening have been calculated at millions to one or even greater.

In 2005, a 12-year-old Ethiopian girl was kidnapped and beaten for days in attempts to force her into an unwanted marriage. Lions chased off her kidnappers and guarded her for half a day. When help arrived, the lions got up and calmly walked off into the forest having completed their part in her rescue.

In 2010, rescuers were still searching for an 11-year-old girl who had been missing for over four days in a Florida swamp. A man from a local church prayed and headed into the swamp. He said he felt God leading him to go straight even when he was surrounded by water. Less than a couple hours later, he found the girl.

In 2011, Annabell Beam was climbing an old tree. It apparently had been decaying on the inside. She fell roughly 30 feet into the trunk of the hollowed out tree. It took five hours to get her out. (Imagine being stuck *inside* a tree for five hours!) This fall ended up being possibly Annabell's greatest blessing. For over four years, Annabell had suffered from an incurable disease, Pseudo Obstruction Motility Disorder. After the tree accident, Annabell's incurable disease was gone.

In January of 2015, 14-year-old John Smith fell through the ice on Lake Sainte Louise. John was underwater for 15 minutes and didn't have a heartbeat for roughly an hour. Mom was encouraged to say her goodbyes. He was clinically dead. But mom prayed, and his heart began to beat. Even once the heartbeat came back, doctors didn't think he'd survive the night. Long story short, John was released 16 days after he fell through the ice and lives a normal life today. (Steph Curry served as an executive producer on the film.)

Two months later in 2015, firefighters and police officers arrived at the Spanish Fork River to a call about an overturned vehicle near the bank. It had been upside down for 13 hours. Once closer, the men heard calls for help from the vehicle. Realizing someone was still alive in the car, the men leapt into action and waded into the frigid water. They responded with reassurances that help was on the way and that they'd get her out safely. With a surge of adrenaline, they managed to flip the wrecked car. They saw 18-month-old baby Lilly in the back seat–her car seat had kept her above the freezing water. Her mom had been deceased for many hours. Afterwards, some of the rescuers were even treated for hypothermia from the cold. As the dust settled and things calmed down, the rescuers had one haunting question: "Who called out for help?" The mom had been dead for hours. Aside from the baby, no one else was in the car, and babies that age don't talk, at least not in a voice like that...

Skeptical? You should be because these tales defy logic and natural laws. Please don't take my word for it; I encourage you to research the validity of each of these stories.

The common denominator in each of these narratives is a loving God moving on behalf of His children. Nearly all are direct responses to prayer. None of these are explainable. Some are scientifically impossible. Others are more improbable than winning the lottery. Each is a miracle in its own right, and there are hundreds, perhaps thousands, more similar stories. These are just a few of the more well-documented ones.

God is real.

You might ask, "Well, what about people who pray and don't get the answer they want?"

That's a great question.

When my dad got cancer about 12 years ago, I prayed and prayed often. He's still alive, cancer free and doing well for a man soon to be 80. When my brother-in-law was found unresponsive in his early

30s, I also prayed, perhaps more. About seven weeks later, we celebrated his life at his funeral service. It was heartbreaking.

I don't have all the answers. God is bigger and smarter than I am. We live in a fallen world.

Evelyn Underhill said it like this, "If God were small enough to be understood, He would not be big enough to be worshiped."

Just look around. People have a tendency to find what they're looking for. What if the next generation quit looking for life outside of God and started looking for Him?

In Chattanooga, you can see seven states from the top of Lookout Mountain. The view is flat out amazing!

Have you ever flown across an ocean? You can fly for hours and see deep blue as far as the horizon in every direction.

Or have you been so far away from civilization on a clear night that when you looked up into the sky, you could see the Milky Way?

Have you snorkeled through the Great Barrier Reef? Have you watched the sun set gloriously over the Kalahari Desert like a magnificent painting? Have you hiked through the Amazon Rain Forest or the Appalachian Trail in the Great Smoky Mountains? Have you cruised through the fjords of Norway? Have you watched the march of the penguins in Antarctica? Have you seen camels cross the Sahara? Have you seen someone go out of their way to sacrifice for another human they don't even know?

If you're looking with open eyes, you can see God in all these things.

God does exist. May you find Him now.

After I had completed this manuscript, finished editing and was in the proofreading process, I came across this meme which seems to have gone viral in various forms across social media. (Some attribute it to John Tyson, but I was unable to find hard evidence of its creator.) The meme summarizes a number of the arguments I made in this chapter, so I will share it.

To be atheist you must believe 6 miracles:

1) order from chaos

2) nothing created everything

3) morals came from matter

4) life from non life

5) reason from non reason

6) personal from non personal.

Skeptics probably take issue with the word "miracles" but what other terminology would you suggest when order, logic, life, emotions, and well everything, comes from... nothing?

Scientifically, the evidence for God is so strong. For one, there's no satisfactory answer for the origin of the universe outside of God. The evidence of His handiwork is everywhere: from the cosmos to your fingerprints, from black holes to DNA, from the top of Mt. Everst to the Mariana Trench. Even human engineers had to go to the divine design of a peregrine falcon's nasal passage to create modern jet engines that wouldn't "choke" under such high speed. It's the only bird that possesses this cone-shaped tubercle bone.

Observationally, there are countless stories of events that can't be explained by natural laws, but can only be explained by the miraculous intervention of God.

Philosophically, nothing outside God gives life meaning.

Sure, buying into the lie that God doesn't exist conveniently allows you to live any way you want to live and do whatever you want to do.

It will also be a very empty life. You might find a lot of pleasure, but you won't find fulfillment. On top of that, it won't be long before those pleasures become old, boring and dull. Often, those "pleasures" turn into burdens of addiction, low self-esteem, STD's, enslaving habits, major health issues, divorce, other broken or damaged relationships, and even death.

Conversely, having a relationship with your Creator will give your life purpose, open your spirit to endless wonder, and bring a sense of satisfaction and fulfillment you can't get anywhere else.

God created you in His image and for His purpose. He loves you. He has a plan for you. He wants to have a personal relationship with you, and He wants to use you to make the world a better place.

That's right. The Creator of the universe wants to know YOU. He's waiting with arms wide open. He's listening. If you don't know where to start, just kneel and pray or grab a Bible and start reading the book of John.

"To suppose that the eye with all its inimitable contrivances for adjusting the focus to different distances, for admitting different amounts of light, and for the correction of spherical and chromatic aberration, could have been formed by natural selection, seems, I freely confess, absurd in the highest degree."
— Charles Darwin (from *The Origin of Species*)

Bonus Chapter
Science Proves There Is No God.

Reread the above quote again.

The Father of Evolution, Charles Darwin, admitted that the eye *alone* made his theories on *The Origin of Species* seem "absurd."

Wow! You have to respect his honesty.

Darwin then spent a couple paragraphs striving to explain how one could rationalize it happening through slight graduations over a vast amount of time.

In fact, Darwin employed this strategy precisely and repeatedly throughout *Origin of Species*, writing multiple chapters listing the obvious objections and major difficulties to his theory on the front end and then addressing them.[1] It was a brilliant plan because in naming such evident holes in his theory on the front end, it gave others less ammo to attack those holes later. Darwin also went to great lengths diving into each issue making challenges so laborious that people easily get lost in the scientific rambling.

Volumes of books have been written in support of and rejection of Darwin's ideas. The average person not only hasn't read these, but hasn't read much, if any, of *The Origin of Species*. And even fewer adequately understand what they have read.

There is no consensus of scientific evidence that definitively proves God's existence; however, there are two separate scientific issues that point toward God indirectly over and over again. Yes, they both revolve around evolution.

Before you roll your eyes (too late maybe), I'm going to challenge you one final time to read open-mindedly. Think critically from a ground zero level as if you've forgotten everything you've been taught and you're exploring the evidence for the first time.

A fascinating example of natural selection occurred in the chilly South Pacific. Although minor details vary among sources, the main factors are the same across multiple accounts.

In 1896, a farmer leased Campbell Island from New Zealand and brought roughly 400 sheep to the island which were sheared seasonally for their wool. The climate was extremely harsh. Direct sunlight was limited. The temperature was frigid, and the wind was fierce. Even the plants were tough to eat due to the harsh conditions. Over time, the population varied, but was roughly 4,000 when it was completely abandoned in 1931. For around 50 years, the herd survived with little to no human contact. No feeding. No medical care. No housing during heavy snows. No sheering whatsoever.

So what happened to the sheep?

As one might guess, the wool grew longer and thicker, but there's more. These sheep also began to self shed during the warmer months. Interestingly, even their legs grew longer. Their jaws and teeth changed from having to pull so hard on the vegetation. Their hooves grew longer. But their evolution was not limited to physical changes only. Behavioral changes such as giving birth while standing up and ewes walking within minutes of being born were the new norm.

226

In about 15 generations and only five decades, natural selection had produced a new breed of sheep. In the context of all time, these documented changes were observed in the blink of an eye.

At first glance, one might think that this sheep study supports the theory of matter-to-man evolution, but as always, let's dig a little deeper.

This study proves that natural selection occurs, and occurs extremely quickly. In fact, all that has been observed in recorded human history is *microevolution*: one species growing longer fur, changes in coloring, having a larger beak, having shorter or longer limbs, resistance to pesticides, etc. Basically, humans have observed, documented and completed experiments proving microevolution again and again and again. However, humans have never observed, recorded or proven one example of *macroevolution* (large scale changes such as from one *kind* to another *kind*).

For instance, cats have a scientific name of felis catus. Dogs are named canis lupus familiaris. We have never observed one of these animal kinds evolving into a different kind. For that matter, no living *taxonomic family* has ever been observed evolving into a different family. Ever!

Furthermore, scientists are realizing that natural selection actually is *not* adding new DNA information, but natural selection often eliminates DNA information. Take, for example, the classic case of peppered moths changing colors. The information of light and dark coloring has been there for thousands of years. As natural selection is occurring, the information of the light colored moths is being lost as more of the darker moths reproduce. (They have better camouflage after the industrial revolution and become prey less often.) DNA

227

information in roaches, bed bugs and bacteria that are becoming resistant to pesticides is not evolving into new genetic code. Those pests that weren't as resistant are dying off, the resistant pests are reproducing and that old genetic code is being lost. Similarly, the same can be observed with mammals that move into much colder or warmer climates. New DNA information is not added to have a more suitable coat; on the contrary, the individuals with less suitable coats tend to be less healthy, reproduce less and their genetic code becomes less and less with each new generation until it is eventually eliminated.

Quick rabbit trail: while on the subject of DNA, how did DNA come about? It has been referred to as genetic information, a code, a protein and a language. Whatever term one uses to describe DNA, its layered complexity is greater than humans can yet begin to comprehend. Is it possible for something so intricately sophisticated to have arisen by random processes over time? Or was there some kind of divine intervention?

Now let's get back to our topic of evolution. There are examples of species changing and interbreeding (closely related species like similar snakes); and this is referred to as speciation. The next classification up from species is genus, and it still remains that one genus has never been observed to evolve into another genus.

Some people will say to look at the fossil record.

You know what hard evidence is there? Fossils. The fossil is proof that a particular animal existed. You know what hard evidence is not in the fossil record? One kind of animal reproducing a different kind.

This macroevolution has *never* been witnessed or documented. It simply has never been proven. In fact, since microevolution has been observed to occur with such rapidity, why does it all of a sudden stop time after time after time, and we never witness the macroevolution?

When I visited the Colosseum, I read where they had found bones of bears, tigers, lions, rhinos, elephants and more under the floor. Those animals died 2,000 years ago. We still have all those same animals today. There is virtually no difference in those those skeletons and the skeletons of the same species today. Since we have documented such great changes in microevolution in a few decades or less, why do we not see a single example of macroevolution in the past 20 centuries, or even longer?

The lack of any concrete evidence of macroevolution change is a major obstacle to the theory of evolution in which skeptics are told just to blindly accept that it happened over billions of years. It is simply irrational to witness such rapid changes that suddenly stop in every single species humans study and accept that we've just never been in the right place at the right time. That is unacceptable science.

It is at this point we should consider the following question: Has there ever been another theory with less concrete evidence, so improbable, so few relevant and repeatable experiments, and with such blind faith as the theory of evolution?

Think about it.

Is there any other theory so widely held as fact with so few or zero complimentary experiments to prove them? Gravity? That's easy. Hold out an object and let go. Sun's effect on your skin? Again, pretty easy. Go to the beach in summer on a cloudless day for a few hours. Water's effect on plants? Water one tomato plant every other day for a month and don't water a second plant for a month.

Are there any repeatable experiments proving one kind of animal changed into another kind, such as a fish to a reptile, a reptile to a bird or an antelope to a giraffe? No.

There are precisely zero repeatable experiments to confirm macroevolution. Additionally, there are zero repeatable experiments to conclusively verify the age of the earth. Coincidentally, despite untold attempts by scientists across the globe, there are also zero experiments that brought about life from a big bang. [The Miller-Urey experiment was the closest. It produced amino acids and the most basic ones at that. However, it didn't produce any life form or anything close (no DNA, no blood, no breath, no reproductive capabilities, no heartbeat, no thought, no emotions, etc.).]

Many people so strongly believe this theory with such little understanding of it, which is rather concerning as well. If you ask for the strongest evidence from the average person who believes that humans evolved from ape-like beings, mammals and birds evolved from reptiles and we all share a common ancestor, you'll get a few similar responses and each is void of concrete evidence (stuff like rock layers, fossil records and genetic mutations).

And what is more worrisome is that in spite of a lack of substantial evidence that the average person can fully understand, if you even question the obvious, gaping holes in evolution (and the big bang), you are mocked and made to feel like an uneducated, idiot who knows nothing about science.

So, what will you find when you really research the evidence for evolution?

First, you'll find that the evidence is surprisingly thin for what you thought was a concrete widely-accepted theory. Second, you will

230

find so much "evidence" that has later been determined to be either fraudulent or flat out wrong.

I want to break this down so even the average high school student can understand many of the basic issues with the story of evolution.

First of all, believing that God created the world takes faith. Some might use the term *miracle*. However, to reiterate a point from the previous chapter one has to have even *more* faith to believe how modern science says we got here and evolved. You need to believe in at least five distinct miracles (naturally impossible or infinitesimally improbable occurrences):

- that a tiny, hot, dense point (a super black hole whose origin remains unexplained) had a "big bang" that started the space-matter-energy-time dimensions of our universe,
- that over billions of years the electrons and quarks created matter in the form of atoms and then mixed with clouds and gasses to form galaxies,
- that these elements mixed at just the right temperature in just the right proportions at precisely the right distances from stars so as not to be too hot or too cold to produce a miniscule life form,
- that this life form didn't die, but instead was able to reproduce,
- that this life form reproduced and evolved into every living thing on our planet, from bacteria to whales, from worms to cedar trees, from birds to beasts, etc.

This is as believable as saying I won a $100 million dollar lottery in Florida, drove to Georgia the same day and won a $100 million dollar lottery, won a $150 million dollar lottery in North

Carolina the next day and a $200 million dollar lottery in Virginia the day after that. This is the theory that students are told, rather indoctrinated with, and expected to believe as fact and ridiculed if they don't.

How much arrogance do we as humans have that we think we know with such certainty what happened supposedly several billion years ago? What solid evidence do we have for the origin of life being this?

None, whatsoever.

It's a theory. So why is it so widely accepted?

Here's why, at least partially.

In 1925, John T. Scopes went on trial for teaching evolution in Dayton, TN. At the time, it was illegal to teach evolution in Tennessee. This became known as "The Monkey Trial" and was the first trial to be broadcast live on radio (TVs wouldn't be common for roughly another 20 years). The country was listening. For eight days as evidence and testimony were presented, defense attorney Clarence Darrow leaned on one key strategy: argue that evolution was science and anyone who disagreed was an illiterate moron who didn't know anything. Newspapers delivered the regular updates of the trial across the globe. It was almost portrayed as the highly educated, world travelling Charles Darwin and his "scientifically proven" theory of evolution vs. the state law of backwoods, ignorant towns in TN.

Darrow's strategy failed in the courtroom (he lost the trial) but won in the court of public opinion. Around that time, the shift in the accepted view of the origin of life and the history of the universe began. It shifted from God and thousands of years to a bang and billions of years. There was no singular key piece of evidence produced

232

at trial that was a catalyst for this change. There was simply a common desire among people not to be seen as uneducated and ignorant.

For the past century and a half, there has been a historical pattern of new scientific discoveries supporting evolution that are later found to be false or misunderstood. The problem is that each new "discovery" is widely and loudly heralded as evidence of evolution, which strengthens popular opinion; however, when said discovery is proven incorrect, the revelation is discreet and quickly forgotten. Often, the discoveries are published in scientific journals, broadcast worldwide through media and written into textbooks. Everyone accepts it. Decades later, when the validity of said "discovery" is legitimately called into question or simply proven false, it is downplayed, put on the back page, ignored or interpreted only in ways that allow for evolution.

Here are just a few examples of how this pattern has unfolded.

In the mid-1800s, Charles Lyell popularized his theory of uniformitarianism which basically states that the geological features steadily and constantly formed over long periods of time.[2] Uniformitarianism was championed by Darwin and accepted widely by scientists and geologists across the globe of how virtually all geological formations were formed. Then, Mount Tarawera erupted, petrifying numerous items in a matter of minutes or days, poor irrigation practices led to the formation of "Georgia's Little Grand Canyon," Mt. St. Helens blew its top 1,300 feet of elevation clear off, creating new lakes in the process, and the island of Surtsey formed. As a result, scientists are now recognizing that catastrophicism (or neocatastrophicism in some circles), the theory that earth was shaped not only by gradual but also by catastrophic events in rather quick processes, had a major role across many places on the planet.

In this same vein, petrification was also believed to have taken millions of years by scientists in the 1800s. However, by the 1980s, scientists could no longer ignore examples across the globe of petrification occurring quickly around hot springs, when organisms are quickly covered in water and silt, and from volcanic eruptions among other processes.

One hundred and fifty years ago, scientists believed that rock layers took millions or at least many, many thousands of years to form. A slew of discoveries, however, have contradicted this notion so much that scientists have backed off their time frame, at least for a number of types of rocks. For instance, there are a number of rock hard layers, one on top of many others, that are all bent but not broken. This can't happen if each took thousands of years to lay down and solidify. The London Hammer is an 1800's hammer encased in a rock that was discovered roughly fifty years after the hammer was made. That rock formed in less than a half century. There are a number of examples of polystrate fossils, particularly fossilized trees which stretch through dozens of rock layers. These suggest that dozens of rock layers can be created in less than the life of a tree, or more likely, less than a few years because the tree would likely die if it were being covered up by rock layer after rock layer.

In 1912, Charles Dawson discovered a new missing link between monkey and man, named Piltdown Man. This infamous "discovery" was determined to be a complete hoax 40 years later. However, for four decades, it was touted as "proof" of evolution, reinforcing popular belief.

Similarly, in 1917, a rancher found a weird fossilized tooth. It was declared to be another missing link, and "Nebraska Man" was born. From a single tooth, sketches of these hominids were drawn, published (including in at least two scientific, peer-reviewed journals) and shared on a large scale. Less than a decade later, the tooth was determined to be from a wild pig; however, since the retraction was less noteworthy, the myth of "Nebraska Man" continued to deceive people long after he was proven nonexistent.

As mentioned previously, in the 1800s, Louis Agassiz touted the coelacanth as a missing transitional link. Charles Darwin approved. From a number of quality fossils, these fishlike creatures with extra appendages clearly allowing them to start to walk on land were obvious transitional creatures to many. The fossil record reveals their demise roughly 65 million years ago. When they were discovered still alive in 1938, it was roughly 50 years after the deaths of Agassiz and Darwin. They, therefore, were unable to share their thoughts on those "extra appendages" that were merely fins. Even more damning, is the fact that the coelacanth appears remarkably similar to the supposed 65 million year old fossils...in other words, there hasn't been any significant evolution in the species over the past supposedly 60 million to 100 million years.

In 1983, *Science* magazine published an article entitled *Origin of Whales in Epicontinental Remnant Seas: New Evidence from the Early Eocene of Pakistan* which claimed pakicetus was a missing link from a land mammal to one of the earliest whales.[3] At that time, all the evidence the authors had was parts of a skull. However, the magazine published a detailed drawing *on the cover* from an artist's imagination depicting a mammal diving into the water after a fish. Roughly twenty years later, an entire skeleton was unearthed and pakicetus was realized to be a simple terrestrial wolf-like creature with zero evidence it spent any time in the water.

Please note: this is a peer reviewed scientific journal! Unfortunately, the scientific community is so eager to produce evidence to corroborate the story of evolution, that they regularly accept unsubstantiated evidence in favor of evolution. They also quickly discount much evidence that challenges evolution.

More recently, in 2005, Mary Schweitzer discovered flexible blood vessels (soft tissue that decomposes) in t-rex bones.[4] Up to this point, scientists were basically unanimous in agreement that due to their age, soft tissue could not possibly exist in dinosaur bones. There's only three possible explanations for the soft tissue:

1. crosscontamination,
2. the dinosaurs lived much more recently than believed, or
3. there is a yet unknown preservation process of soft tissue for millions of years.

After finding more examples of soft tissue in dinosaur bones eliminating the first possibility, many scientists disregarded the second option and readily embraced the third possibility as the only option (because a young earth doesn't fit their preconceived idea of millions of years). What was unanimously accepted 20 years ago, no soft tissue in dinosaur bones, flipped in a few short years to protect the belief in billions of years.

Even more recently, scientists have run into an even greater blow to the theory that dinosaurs died out millions of years ago when they started finding collagen in numerous dinosaur remains. The problem is that scientific studies have determined that collagen is a fragile protein that decays quickly and could in all realistic probability only last a few thousand years under the most ideal conditions. Evolutionists have to either abandon their belief in the age of the earth or abandon their belief in the decay rate of collagen. Since most scientists never even question their belief in the age of the earth and always alter any contradicting scientific findings, evolutionary scientists are now desperately trying to explain how the collagen has been preserved.

While on the subject of dinosaurs, it's interesting to note that roughly 100 separate ancient cultures have stories of huge serpent-like creatures. Many of these have lasting depictions of long-necked animals resembling dinosaurs. Either this is a baffling coincidence or a few thousand years ago, people actually saw dinosaurs. Nowadays, we refer to these reports as "dragon myths" (because we are so much smarter than those ancient cultures, of course). It's also curious that the Chinese have identified 12 spirit animals: each is a living animal we still have today, except the dragon. Why did the ancient Chinese include eleven real live animals and one fake animal? Could it be possible that dinosaurs existed a few thousand years ago and humans saw them? I'm not saying it definitely happened. I'm just asking if it's possible.

Science is supposed to be all about observations, discovery, experiments and learning new ways the world works; however, you will not find theories with more staunch deniability than the concept that the earth might be younger than we thought and evolution might not be the mechanism that produced all the various life forms on earth. It doesn't matter what discoveries are made, many people will never entertain the possibility that their thoughts on an old earth and their thoughts on evolution just maybe could be wrong.

Darwin himself attempted to address the issue of lack of missing links in the fossil record writing "...as this process of extermination has acted on an enormous scale, so must the number of intermediate varieties, which have formerly existed, be truly enormous. Why then is not every geological formation and every stratum full of such intermediate links? Geology assuredly does not reveal any such finely-graduated organic chain; and this, perhaps, is the most obvious and serious objection which can be urged against the theory."[1]

He also wrote, "That the geological record is imperfect all will admit," and, "He who rejects this view of the imperfection of the geological record, will rightly reject the whole theory."[1]

Here we are 150 years later, and with modern science and technology, scientists should be asking more questions about why the fossil record is so insufficient when it comes to transitional forms. Humans have now uncovered billions of fossils. This baffling number of missing links can only be overlooked by people whose bias allows them to accept evolution despite the dearth of fossil evidence.

For the third time, the "living fossil" coelacanth was one of the best examples of a missing link until we learned it is still alive and it's not a link at all. This discovery should also make mankind question how confident we should realistically be in studying fossils from past millenia when we have proven our theories of them can be so wrong. Unfortunately, scientists who have predetermined that evolution is the only possibility, won't ask these obvious questions.

Koalas, which supposedly evolved extremely far away from humans on the evolutionary tree, have the closest fingerprints to humans (not our closest supposed living relative, the chimpanzee) of all species. What are the chances that two species evolving separately over millions of years would evolve fingerprints so similar that even forensic experts have trouble distinguishing them?

Pandas appear to be not much different from other bears, but there are distinctions. Most notably, they don't eat *any* meat. They eat bamboo. Their stomachs, however, are not like ruminids, so they spend the large majority of every day eating bamboo, which contains cyanide by the way, to fulfill their caloric needs. They are known for being clumsy, rolling in manure and pooping 40 times a day. According to the common sense of natural selection, this animal would *never* have evolved.

Evolutionists talk a lot about how a giraffe's elongated neck is evidence of evolving to reach food high in the trees; however, the fossil record lacks gradual evolution of this species. There are some fossils of extinct species such as canthumeryx, but even this is closer to a horse than a giraffe. There should be scores of transitional forms to get to a giraffe, but these links remain missing. Why?

Hummingbirds from their size to the way they fly to their beaks to their diet are completely unlike any other birds and yet look exactly the same in the fossil record from supposedly millions of years ago. The great many transitional forms for this tiny and adorable bird simply don't exist in the fossil record.

Other animals whose mere existence outright challenges the plausibility of evolution include the aardvark, pangolin, kakapo, hoatzin, horseshoe crab, goblin shark, aye-aye and platypus.

By this point, one might have thought about Neanderthals. I recently visited the Smithsonian Natural Museum of History, and I was personally in awe of the difference between a normal human skull and a Neanderthal skull. But then something happened, as I got to the panels where the most recent human skulls were on display, I realized there was almost just as much difference between two of the recent human skulls as there was between an assumed old Neanderthal skull and a recent human skull. This means that just because the shape, size or color is different doesn't mean that it is for sure a different kind of beast. After reflection, it occurred to me that there are bound to be significant differences today in the skull of an eskimo who eats mostly meat, a woman in the Amazon who eats a lot of fruit and a bushman in the Khalihari Desert whose diet is anything he can find and who consumes a fraction of water of the others.

But I may be biased on the issue, so don't take it from me.

Evolutionist and perhaps the foremost authority on Neanderthals Erik Trinkaus said, "Detailed comparisons of Neanderthal skeletal remains with those of modern humans have shown that there is nothing in Neanderthal anatomy that conclusively indicates locomotor, manipulative, intellectual or linguistic abilities inferior to those of modern humans."[5]

To paraphrase, he's basically saying that there is not nearly as much difference between the skeletons of modern humans and skeletons of "Neanderthals" as most people think.

Another common suggestion that the average person will provide as proof of evolution is Carbon-14 (i.e. radiocarbon) dating. The constant rate of isotopes is taught in schools, but most people don't have a full understanding of these dating methods. For starters, Carbon-14 itself has a very short half life, meaning it should be completely gone in thousands of years; therefore, it is completely

240

useless to date objects that are supposed to be millions of years old. Scientists then use other elements with longer half lives to date objects that they consider older.

There are a number of problems with these dating methods. First, Carbon-14 is often found in dinosaur bones. This should not be possible if they are millions of years old. Evolutionists explain this away by suggesting other natural processes contaminated the sample by adding the carbon to things after they are dead. However, if bones, or even rock layers, can be contaminated/altered by natural processes, then how valid are these dating methods? These scientists are basically saying that certain examples fit their timeline, so they are legit, but other examples (such as dinosaur bones with carbon) don't fit their timeline, so these are not legit. That's selective reasoning. One can't have it both ways. Also, scientists are running into problems dating things whose date they are actually sure of like the mortar in the Colosseum. Scientists know roughly when the Colosseum and other historic structures were built, yet they are getting inaccurate dates of the substances used in their construction with standard dating methods.[6]

Just let all this element dating method stuff sink in for a minute. …if Carbon-14 can be added to old dinosaur bones, isn't it logical that other elements such as uranium, potassium and hafnium can be added to old bones as well? If so, then won't that make these dating methods invalid or, at least, unreliable?

To the average person? Yes.

To the scientists whose entire life's work is tied to his core belief in evolution? Unfortunately, they will only interpret any and all evidence in a way that fits their preconceived idea of billions of years.

Summary

After reviewing the history of the theory of evolution, the evidence for evolution that has been determined false, incomplete or misinterpreted, and more recent *objective* scientific observations, an unbiased reader must admit two things.

First, major questions and issues about the age of the earth persist. Why are we, then, so forcefully told the universe is billions of years old and dinosaurs lived millions of years ago? Is there a worldview that is biasing the way the data has been interpreted? What does the evidence say in of itself?

With recent discoveries in the fossilization process, rapid petrification, errors in isotope dating methods and examples of rocks forming more quickly than assumed last century, it is only prudent and reasonable to recognize that the earth might be younger than we've been told.

Secondly, there is no hard evidence that macroevolution has occurred or has occurred on such a gargantuan level as to produce all life on earth as we know it. Since microevolution through natural selection has been observed with so many species and with such rapidity across the globe, why hasn't anyone in all of recorded history ever been able to observe or document one genus changing into another and producing offspring of this new genus? Why does the evolution process always abruptly stop in front of our eyes at the micro before the macro? One has to consider the possibility that although minor changes occur within a genus, perhaps animals without exoskeletons don't sprout them, animals with two eyes don't grow more eyes (a would be helpful adaptation for all of us), and animals that can't fly, don't grow wings and feathers, light skeletons, highly efficient respiratory systems, feet to stand on branches, talons to catch prey, and keen eyesight simultaneously along the evolutionary tree to to enable the ability to fly.

The truth is that the theory of evolution is not as much of a scientific, evidenced-based, experiment-tested theory as it is an alternative to a divine being creating the universe theory. There is a mountain of evidence and scientific reason that points toward a young earth and also that indicates one beast doesn't evolve into another kind, family or genus of beast. The small sample of that evidence and logic that was presented in this final chapter should be enough to open an unbiased reader to those possibilities. However, those possibilities come with a major implication. First, if the earth is less than a million years old, then the evolutionary time frame is 100% impossible. Also, if the animals do not evolve from one genus to another, then how did they get here? Who created them? If either of these two things are true—a young earth or that macroevolution doesn't occur—then one has no other alternative but to consider supernatural intervention in the formation of our universe and the creation of life.

May God bless you, guide you and show you the wonders of His world.

Notes

Introduction
1. Reiner, Rob. *A Few Good Men*. Columbia Pictures, 1992.
2. Storytelling.co.za. "The Naked Truth and the Lie." *Storytelling.co.za*. Accessed August 11, 2024. https://storytelling.co.za/the-naked-truth-and-the-lie.

Chapter 2: *You're worthless.*
1. Tenth Avenue North. "You Are More." On *The Light Meets the Dark*. Reunion Records, April 27, 2010.
2. *The Butterfly Circus*. Directed by Joshua Weigel. Performances by Eduardo Verástegui and Nick Vujicic. Peacetree Productions, 2009.
3. Vujicic, Nick. *Nick Vujicic: Home*. Nick Vujicic. Accessed July 17, 2025. https://nickvujicic.com.
4. Vujicic, Nick. *Life Without Limits: Inspiration for a Ridiculously Good Life*. New York: Crown Archetype, 2010.

Chapter 3: *You can't.*
1. Colbert, Stephen. "Mary J. Blige and Alison Roman." *The Late Show with Stephen Colbert*. Season 8, episode 93. CBS, March 28, 2023.
2. *"List of Awards and Nominations Received by Mary J. Blige."* *Wikipedia, The Free Encyclopedia*. Last revised May 6, 2025. https://en.wikipedia.org/wiki/List_of_awards_and_nominations_received_by_Mary_J._Blige.
3. *A Million Miles Away*. Directed by Alejandra Márquez Abella. Performances by Michael Peña and Garret Dillahunt. Amazon MGM Studios/Select Films, 2023. Amazon Prime Video.
4. *The Holy Bible: King James Version*. Thomas Nelson, 1987. Psalm 139:14.

Chapter 4: *You deserve a nice meal.*
1. Daughtry, Chris, and Brett Sandquist. *Home*. On *Daughtry*. RCA Records, 2006.
2. Zeballos, Eliana, and Wilson Sinclair. "Total Food Spending

Reached $2.63 Trillion in 2024." *USDA Economic Research Service*, Accessed June 10, 2025. https://www.ers.usda.gov.

3. Dundes, Lauren, and Jeff Marx. "Balancing Work and Academics in College: Why Do Students Working 10 to 19 Hours per Week Excel?" *Journal of College Student Retention* 8, no. 1 (2006–2007): 107–120.

Chapter 5: *OPM is the secret to getting rich.*

1. Page, Andrew. "Paycheck-to-Paycheck Statistics." *MarketWatch*. Accessed September 2, 2024.
https://www.marketwatch.com/financial-guides/banking/paycheck-to-p aycheck-statistics/.

Chapter 6: *At some point, you will have to grow up.*

1. *"Travis King."* Wikipedia: The Free Encyclopedia. Wikimedia Foundation. Accessed August 23, 2024.
https://en.wikipedia.org/wiki/Travis_King.

Chapter 7: *Racism isn't much of an issue any more.*

1. Lee, Harper. *To Kill a Mockingbird*. Philadelphia: J. B. Lippincott & Co., 1960.

2. *Just Mercy*. Directed by Destin Daniel Cretton. Performances by Michael B. Jordan, Jamie Foxx, and Brie Larson. Burbank, CA: Warner Bros. Pictures, 2019.

3. *A Bronx Tale*. Directed by Robert De Niro. Performances by Robert De Niro and Chazz Palminteri. Savoy Pictures, 1993.

4. *Ghosts of Mississippi*. Directed by Rob Reiner. Performances by Alec Baldwin, Whoopi Goldberg, and James Woods. Columbia Pictures, 1996.

5. *42*. Directed by Brian Helgeland. Performances by Chadwick Boseman, Harrison Ford, and Nicole Beharie. Warner Bros. Pictures, 2013.

6. *Selma*. Directed by Ava DuVernay. Performances by David Oyelowo, Tom Wilkinson, Carmen Ejogo, and Oprah Winfrey. Paramount Pictures, 2014.

7. *Hidden Figures*. Directed by Theodore Melfi. Performances by Taraji P. Henson, Octavia Spencer, Janelle Monáe, Kevin Costner, and

Kirsten Dunst. 20th Century Fox, 2016.

8. *Green Book*. Directed by Peter Farrelly. Performances by Viggo Mortensen and Mahershala Ali. Universal Pictures, 2018.

9. *The Best of Enemies*. Directed by Robin Bissell. Performances by Taraji P. Henson and Sam Rockwell. STX Films, 2019.

10. *Till*. Directed by Chinonye Chukwu. Performances by Danielle Deadwyler and Jalyn Hall. United Artists Releasing, 2022.

Chapter 8: *The government will take care of you.*
1. *The Constitution of the United States: A Transcription.* National Archives and Records Administration. September 17, 1787. https://www.archives.gov/founding-docs/constitution-transcript.

2. Coursera Staff. "Is Community College Free? (In Some States, Yes)." *Coursera.* Last updated November 29, 2023. https://www.coursera.org/articles/is-community-college-free.

Chapter 9: *Racism in America hasn't improved.*
1. *The Gospel According to Mac.* Directed by Jim Podhoretz. ESPN Films, November 3, 2015. Television documentary.

Chapter 10: *You need to have your phone on you (for emergencies).*
1. Kaminyar, Kevin. "Is Social Media Making You Less Social? In a Time When We Seem More Social, We Are Also Lonely and Disconnected." *Entrepreneur*, March 14, 2023.

2. Evans, Jeremy. "The Dawn of Digital Relationships." *Highlands Marriage Conference*, February 24–25, 2023.

Chapter 11: *There are some things you don't have to forgive.*
1. Dunn, Warrick, and Don Yaeger. *Running for My Life: My Journey in the Game of Football and Beyond.* New York: HarperCollins, 2008.

2. Evans, Jeremy. "The Dawn of Digital Relationships." *Highlands Marriage Conference*, February 24–25, 2023.

3. Johns Hopkins Medicine. "Forgiveness: Your Health Depends on It." Johns Hopkins Medicine, Johns Hopkins University. Accessed July 2, 2025.

https://www.hopkinsmedicine.org/health/wellness-and-prevention/forgi
veness-your-health-depends-on-it.

Chapter 12: *Toxic internal lies.*
1. Flame, featuring NF. *Start Over*. Royal Flush, Clear Sight Music,
2013.

Chapter 13: They *are bad people.*
1. Lazarus, Emma. "The New Colossus." National Park Service, U.S.
Department of the Interior. Accessed December 29, 2024.
https://www.nps.gov/stli/learn/historyculture/colossus.htm.

Chapter 16: *Yes.*
1. "Charles Barkley on His Friendship With Michael Jordan." 60
Minutes. Season 55, episode 23. Directed by Jon Wertheim. CBS,
March 26, 2023.
2. Morabito, Charlotte. "Here's Why Even Americans Making More
Than $100,000 Live Paycheck to Paycheck." CNBC, December 11,
2023.
https://www.cnbc.com/2023/12/11/why-even-americans-making-more-t
han-100000-live-paycheck-to-paycheck.html.

Chapter 17: *You can't argue with science.*
1. National Center for Science Education. "Definitions of Fact, Theory,
and Law in Scientific Work." March 16, 2016.
https://ncse.ngo/definitions-fact-theory-and-law-scientific-work.
2. Buckley, Don, Zipporah Miller, Michael J. Padilla, Kathryn
Thornton, and Michael E. Wysession. *Interactive Science. Middle
School, Grade 6*. Glenview, IL: Pearson, 2019.
3. Corbley, Andy. "Analysis Shows We've Been Overestimating the
Amount of Plastic in Oceans by 30×." *Good News Network*, August 9,
2023.
https://www.goodnewsnetwork.org/analysis-shows-weve-been-overesti
mating-the-amount-of-plastic-in-oceans-by-30x/.

Chapter 18: *Life is fair.*

1. Waterson, Bill. *The Essential Calvin and Hobbes: A Calvin and Hobbes Treasury.* Kansas City, MO: Andrews McMeel Publishing, 1988.

Chapter 19: *The American dream is dead.*
1. Ehrenreich, Barbara. *Nickel and Dimed: On (Not) Getting By in America.* New York: Metropolitan Books, 2001.
2. Ehrenreich, Barbara. *Bait and Switch: The (Futile) Pursuit of the American Dream.* New York: Metropolitan Books, 2005.
3. Shepard, Adam. *Scratch Beginnings: Me, $25, and the Search for the American Dream.* New York: Collins, 2008.
4. Francis, Emily. *If You Only Knew: Letters from an Immigrant Teacher.* Seidlitz Education, September 1, 2022.

Chapter 20: *Successful people don't have real issues.*
1. *Rocky Balboa.* Directed by Sylvester Stallone. Performances by Sylvester Stallone, Burt Young, and Antonio Tarver. Metro-Goldwyn-Mayer (MGM), 2006.

Chapter 21: *Everybody gets student loans.*
1. O'Neal, Anthony. *Debt-Free Degree: The Step-by-Step Guide to Getting Your Kid Through College Without Student Loans.* Nashville: Ramsey Press, 2019.
2. Melanie Hanson, "Average Time to Pay Off Student Loans [2025]: Data Analysis," EducationData.org, accessed July 22, 2025, https://educationdata.org/average-time-to-repay-student-loans.
3. Dave Ramsey (@DaveRamsey), "Your future wealth depends on the decisions you make today," X post, June 17, 2023, 8:45 a.m., accessed July 22, 2025, https://x.com/DaveRamsey/status/1779892636565840092.
4. Hahn, Alicia. "2023 Student Loan Debt Statistics: Average Student Loan Debt." *Forbes Advisor*, 2023. Accessed July 22, 2025. https://www.forbes.com/advisor/student-loans/average-student-loan-debt-statistics/.
5. Ramsey Solutions, *Borrowed Future: How Student Loans Are Killing the American Dream*, directed by David DiCicco (Franklin, TN:

Ramsey Solutions, 2021), streaming video,
https://www.borrowedfuture.com/.

Chapter 22: *No matter what, always have your family's back.*
1. *The Godfather Part II*. Directed by Francis Ford Coppola. Paramount
Pictures, 1974.

Chapter 23: *Everybody's doing it.*
1. Institute for Family Studies. "Less Marriage, Worse Mental Health:
The 'Marriage Advantage' in Mental Well-Being." *Institute for Family
Studies (blog)*, May 15, 2025. Accessed July 22, 2025.
https://ifstudies.org/blog/less-marriage-worse-mental-health-the-marria
ge-advantage-in-mental-well-being.
2. Shmerling, R. J. (2016, November 30). *The health advantages of
marriage*. *Harvard Heal*th Blog. Harvard Health Publishing. Retrieved
from
https://www.health.harvard.edu/blog/the-health-advantages-of-marriage
-2016113010667
3. Kiecolt-Glaser, Janice K., and Tamara L. Newton. "Marriage and
Health: His and Hers." *Psychological Bulletin* 127, no. 4 (2001):
472–503.
4. Cohen, Ilene Strauss. 2017. "The Benefits of Delaying
Gratification." *Psychology Today*, December 26, 2017. Reviewed by
Ekua Hagan. Accessed July 23, 2025.
https://www.psychologytoday.com/us/blog/your-emotional-meter/2017
12/the-benefits-delaying-gratification

Chapter 24: *Lies about abortion.*
1. Covey, Stephen R. *The 7 Habits of Highly Effective People:
Powerful Lessons in Personal Change*. New York: Free Press, 1989.

Chapter 25: *Counseling is for the weak-minded.*
1. Dunn, Warrick, and Don Yaeger. *Running for My Life: My Journey in
the Game of Football and Beyond*. New York: It Books (an imprint of
HarperCollins), 2008.

2. Gray, John. *Men Are from Mars, Women Are from Venus: A Practical Guide for Improving Communication and Getting What You Want in Your Relationships*. New York: HarperCollins, 1992.

3. Tannen, Deborah. *You Just Don't Understand: Women and Men in Conversation*. New York: Ballantine Books, 1990.

Chapter 26: *There's not much difference between boys and girls.*

1. No Longer Fatherless. "Statistics — No Longer Fatherless." Accessed July 24, 2025. https://www.nolongerfatherless.org/statistics.

2. Fatherless Boys Foundation, Inc. "About Us." *Fatherless Boys Foundation*. Accessed July 24, 2025. https://fatherlessboysfoundation.org/about-us.

3. America First Policy Institute. "Fact Sheet | Fatherhood and Crime." *America First Policy Institute*. June 25, 2024. Accessed July 24, 2025. https://www.americafirstpolicy.com/issues/fact-sheet-fatherhood-and-crime.

4. Hurd, Sherrie A. A.A. "7 Painful Psychological Effects of Growing Up Without a Mother." *Learning-Mind*, published two years ago. Accessed July 24, 2025. https://www.learning-mind.com/growing-up-without-a-mother/.

Chapter 27: *There is no God.*

1. Gray, Sarah. Nov 4, 2017. Cosmologist Lawrence Krauss: Religion could be largely gone in a generation. https://www.salon.com/2014/11/04/cosmologist_lawrence_krauss_religion_could_be_largely_gone_in_a_generation/

2. *The Holy Bible: King James Version*. Thomas Nelson, 1987. Matthew 5:38-40.

3. Nagel, Thomas. *The Last Word*. New York: Oxford University Press, 1997.

Bonus chapter for Nerds.

1. Darwin, Charles. *On the Origin of Species by Means of Natural Selection, or the Preservation of Favoured Races in the Struggle for Life*. London: John Murray, 1859.

2. Lyell, Charles. *Principles of Geology: Being an Attempt to Explain the Former Changes of the Earth's Surface, by Reference to Causes Now in Operation*. 3 vols. London: John Murray, 1830–1833.

3. Gingerich, Philip D., M. Mahmood Raza, Muhammad Arif, M. Sabir, and Ishtiaq H. Khan. "Origin of Whales in Epicontinental Remnant Seas: New Evidence from the Early Eocene of Pakistan." *Science* 220, no. 4595 (1983): 403–406.

4. Mary H. Schweitzer et al., "Soft-Tissue Vessels and Cellular Preservation in *Tyrannosaurus rex*," *Science* 307, no. 5717 (2005): 1952–55.

5. Tattersall, Ian. (1995). *The Fossil Trail: How We Know What We Think We Know About Human Evolution*. Oxford University Press.

6. Pesce, Giovanni. 2023. "The Need for a New Approach to the Radiocarbon Dating of Historic Mortars." *Radiocarbon* 65, no. 5 (October): 1017–1021. https://doi.org/10.1017/RDC.2023.92.

www.ingramcontent.com/pod-product-compliance
Lightning Source LLC
Chambersburg PA
CBHW021027130626
46552CB00005B/1720